21st Century Prophets

21st Century Prophets

The Sage Within

GURU SINGH

Guru Singh -- born in 1945 -- is a third-generation yoga master, and master teacher of Kundalini Yoga, Meditation, Mantra and Humanology. He is also a musician, composer, author, artist and Minister of Sikh Dharma. He is based in Los Angeles, Seattle and around the world. Born into a yogic household, he met Yogi Bhajan in January of 1969 and has been teaching, from this ancient Kundalini lineage, throughout the world, ever since. He began studying Western music at the age of five, and Eastern music captured his attention at nineteen . . . his classes are filled with music and mantra -- yoga and meditation -- wit and wisdom. He has published many books and mantra albums . . . you can find his lectures, music and books online at www.gurusingh.com. His daily prayer posts are on Twitter, Instagram and Facebook.

Editor in Chief:
Guruperkarma Kaur

Cover Design:
Kendall Alexis Guilburt (photograph & design)
Arvind Singh (layout & design)

Back Cover Design:
Arvind Singh (layout & design)
Marc Royce (photograph)

Creative and Production Design
Arvind Singh

Produced by ReEvolution Books — A division of Guru Singh Inc. ®
© Guru Singh Inc. ® 2017
ISBN-13: 9781545346075
ISBN-10: 1545346070

Dedication

This book is dedicated to the teachers who keep teaching through life-times and in the dreamtime -- always there in the realities of the moments -- not consumed by the thoughts and comments from a wandering mind. This is the dedication of that everlasting relationship between a teacher and a student -- the master and the disciple -- a relationship that's been existing since life persisted on any planet, in any system, within any galaxy, of any universe. This book is dedicated to all teachers who assume this role without self-interest, and with the complete integrity to pass on their teachings. This book is dedicated to those who have mastered life over the vast fabrics of spacetime -- through the generations -- to enable life to be alive and sustainable growing forward. This book is dedicated to all of these teachers, and to one of these teachers . . . Yogi Bhajan.

Foreword

The subtle energies around this Earth are currently experiencing a massive shift. As sensitive and intuitive beings, you are experiencing this shift as a "fire" more than ever. This "burning" is a blessing, for as you melt and merge, you arrive at your destiny renewed. These are the fires of transmutation, cleansing, and clearing away the brush that no longer serves the grandness of your mission.

You are made of light, it's your nature to burn. You came from the stars, and to the stars you'll return. You are a universe unto yourself -- with every awakening, a new Earth is birthed within you. You are 'The Philosopher's Stone' of this very moment in time. It's your blessing and responsibility, as an enlightened angel, to elevate and nurture all of humanity . . . to deliver peace, and prosperity . . . to reimagine what it means to be human. You are here to redefine the human experience with compassion for all of humanity.

And when there's nothing left to burn . . . you must set your soul on fire. Do not fear the fire, seek those who fan the flames.

Love and Blessings, Kendall Alexis Guilburt
April 12, 2017

Chapters

Sailing the winds of gravity through realms of opportunity is the future pathway for impossibilities to become possible. You'll travel these winds to solve dilemmas of the present with skills from the future . . . you'll work in miracles. These are the mental frequencies that Guru Nanak and the other Sikh Gurus; Lord Buddha; Prophet Mohammed; Lord Krishna, and Lord Jesus -- amongst countless others -- all lived in. They were human, just like you, but they had disciplined their bodies, minds, and senses to capture the faint winds of levity, in any moment at will. It's on these winds they'd sail the vast oceans of life with deep love and joy . . . even in the times of great anguish. Now, those same times of great anguish are again on Earth, and any form of blame completely misses the mark. It's moments like these when supreme lightness and levity are required . . . like walking on water; like healing with the touch of your hands; like the moving of mountains across desert sands; like the sailing with the winds of gravity on carpets of unimaginable magic . . . this is the lightness of levity. You're the new prophets in a world being destroyed by profits . . . a false measure whose value is failing. Things do fall apart when no one's leading the way, and right now it's your turn to lead . . . no one else is. Because you've not yet accepted your authority to accompany your great wisdom, this causes you anguish, but anguish is the sign that your time has arrived. It's time to no longer wait back in line . . . it's time to wake up, rise up, and step up to this time. The clarions are sounding, the angels are calling . . . there's no time to wait, and no one to tell you to go. Tesla and Einstein saw into this future . . . the lightness and space inside the weight of the atom. This is the path of all the great masters of mastery, turning on the lights that eliminate mystery. The leaders of the mystery-version of life are now the 'out-of-control' bullies, with the scapegoats that they've created with centuries of ruthless pillage and rampage. Our prayer is that you'll answer the prayers of the angels; that you'll accept the prophecy of you being you; that you don't wait in line, and don't lag behind, but step into your role as a master who's mastered this time . . . many times.

Time is a memory bank -- it holds the moments that've passed, and the ones that have yet to arrive. The present is created by the moments chosen with, or without consciousness . . . any moment can become now. The only question is, are you going to live in the past, or move life into the future? Those designing a world of massive restrictions are living in the past, and when this becomes systemic, there is no future . . . all systems of service begin to collapse . . . including nature. Today we have this reversal within many powerful nations, these reversals are connected through layers, and they then make the past more compelling than the future . . . time moves backward. When time moves backward for too long, all systems of time stop serving life . . . life runs out of time. Everyone's heard the saying, "Time is money." Money is an energy that's directed by the passage of time. When time moves backward, money jams up into hoards -- it stops serving life -- it begins being used to avoid, or cause death . . . war becomes commonplace. This is the sole result of hoarding and controlling. Money was meant to be like the breath -- available when life needed to inhale. When time runs backward -- people begin to suffocate -- money is no longer an objective servant, it's an object of worship. Under this spell of worshipping money, nothing is served . . . the greediest claim a massive amount . . . the majority receive mere scraps. This is the world today in a disaster of time running in reverse . . . the physical and mental worlds have lost 'vitality' . . . they're collapsing with emotional debris. In the physical world it's stagnation and disease; in the psycho-emotional world it's fear, rage, and depression . . . all are pandemic right now. Our prayer is that you break into the bank of time; take hold of the big clock and reverse its hands, and begin time moving forward again. You'll have to give it forward -- or forgive, as it's commonly known -- and for this you must have the courage of forever . . . the largest measure of time's possibilities. Go ahead -- take the courage -- break into time -- forgive it all -- now pass it forward . . . tag you're it.

*I*t's in the higher dimensions of life's possibilities, the realms you've known in star-systems beyond the horizons of this universe, ones that contain answers to the challenges this Earth faces in this moment, this is where you understand your immortal authority. The current disastrous ecology, disgraceful economics, unrepresentative politics, unrealistic religious intolerances, and disrespectful cultural attitudes are the simple indicators of a sublimation that faces life here on Earth. These attitudes are clearly insulting . . . led by leaders who are scared little children, snarling from positions of complete ignorance, embarrassed to admit they haven't a clue. Identical to the antics of children afraid to learn, because it admits they don't already know -- if you spend any psycho-emotional energy being disgusted, you're completely missing the point and purpose of your life. From higher dimensions you've saved many planets in lifetimes you don't completely remember . . . some in worse shape than Earth. The last of your incarnations have been on these assignments around the multiverse, and the characters being played by the current leaders on Earth, are like the thousands of characters you've faced many times before. When you don't separate from these characters acting badly, but unite with their pain, you acknowledge the connection that exists -- this trains them to do the same. With this union (original meaning of yoga), you engage your brain's lucid, theta state; your body relaxes into ease; your efforts become effortless, and your emotions transform into devotions. You recall the unimaginable ways you've succeeded before . . . the previous incarnations come back to this time with super powers . . . your immortal authority. Our prayer is that you step away from all linear thinking . . . stand outside your normal stance; change your education to raise the new future that performs magic beyond logic. Remember you've done this before, so walk as if you can, and step into those spaces that are not yet occupied, then access the solutions that don't yet exist . . . you'll need to believe that you own them, then own the need to share them.

The gut brain is the teacher of mystics and intuitives; the heart brain is the teacher of masters and compassionates; the head brain is the teacher of the intelligent sentinels, the heroes, but also the thieves. The sentinels are confusing this world with their two dimensional rules of limitations. The heroes are working feverishly to enforce these rules. The thieves are stepping into positions of false authority; recreating the rules in their favor; pillaging the three dimensions of space, and stealing the fourth dimension of everyone's time. The ultimate result is that humans on Earth are running out of time and could be dancing on the threshold of extinction. This is the disaster evolution of life has arrived at on this planet, and humans here are operating at one of the lowest possible levels of human existence. But, you've arrived here on Earth as a witness to this mess -- and you're not just the witness -- you possess a powerful ability to transform the future and fulfill a destiny. There are planets in other star-systems within this Universe and far beyond it . . . star-systems where human life is millions, even billions of years more advanced than it is here. These are the systems that you've lived in and are sent from -- sent here to this planet in its moment of cataclysmic crisis. You know the higher dimensions of life that are possible, but you've been in this planet's mess for so long that you've almost forgotten your assignment. The limitations, doubts and corruptions of the sentinels, heroes and thieves are extremely contagious. You're a master of the heart's connections -- the gut's hunches, and you know the traps of the contagious two dimensional comparisons, competitions, and wars. You know that life, when lived for profit and advantage, becomes a total loss with complete disadvantage. You know this, but you've nearly forgotten. Our prayer is that you remember the authority that goes with your wisdom, and then acknowledge that you're the one with wisdom . . . not the only one, but one of the ones with authority to break through the limits; discount the thieves, and change human destiny. You're the one and right now is the time.

*Y*ou create the fourth dimension of time out of your experi- ence of three dimensions through the filters and sensations that register in memory. This memory then experiences the next moment and the next. To pass through moments clearly and with- out any distortion is known as 'crystal consciousness'. The word was 'Khrysthal' in the ancient Aramaic of Biblical times. This is where the word 'Khryst' -- now spelled Christ -- comes from. This is Christ consciousness; this is Krishna consciousness; this is what Buddha's consciousness is . . . the enlightened and awak- ened birthright of every human life. This awareness is absolutely crystal clear; it carries no memory, or filters . . . it holds intuition as its guiding force, and relies on filter/memory free views of each moment to detect the undefined, undescribed accuracy of the moment. This is what pure faith is . . . it enters every moment without memory -- relying on the intuition to construct a reality of what is in the moment. As you contemplate this 'Khryst' -- the master within you, that's always been with you -- just realize that the only time you can relate to this is when you have the faith. Sometimes put your two hands over your heart and breathe con- sciously, without being the breather . . . close your eyes and go inside . . . find the Christ, that is you, the "I am" that has been there forever. This will give you confidence in the midst of the turbulence of the tyrants that are scavenging the Earth . . . lost and afraid in this very moment. They're waiting for you to lead the way out of their chaos and corruption. Doubt is the only con- tagious disease that stops this ability and replaces it with the dis- torting filters and memories that are relied upon to feel safe. But this safety is the most dangerous place to live . . . it's ultimately lost in three dimensional darkness. This is the current disease of doubt. Our prayer is that you are that Khrysthal consciousness . . . you are that Christ, and that you realize this without exclusivity, but include everyone in this same capacity of doubt-free awareness. This creates the 'tyrant-free' future that's in you . . . it's in every one of you.

Newton's third law of motion – "every action has an equal and opposite reaction" -- is a law that governs all physical matter above the level of the quantum. This has allowed evolution to persist throughout time, and for unwanted dominance to give way to wiser moments. Within the boundaries of this universal law, there's a comforting fact that has repeated throughout history: tyrants inspire urgency; tyrants inspire genius; tyrants inspire a collective enthusiasm, and all of this combines to ultimately overthrow the dominance of tyrants for wiser ideas. This is the pendulum swinging; the tipping point tipping; the leverage that allows evolution to not only survive . . . but to thrive. And we're all aware of the fact that tyrants are in the house right now. For this reason it's now time for you to get in touch with your initial mission of existence, and to find the inner permit for this mission. Combine these two words -- permit and mission -- and you get the 'permission' you need . . . you were born with. You came here to express your genius, and to express the value contained in your inspiration. Valuable is what you represent in every breath . . . called presence, it's not what you live to achieve . . . it's what you already are. This is yours to insist upon; this is what the equal and opposite pushes up against. Tyrants are on the loose and your sense of urgency is sensing this. Allow genius to answer this call of urgency; go into the depth of your meditations and discover the inspiration . . . you're in the middle of creation at its best. Creation is the impulse of the Universe -- a constant forward motion correcting every imbalance. Today, human life hangs in the balance of your ability to access your genius, and inspiration. This is what you're experiencing every day right now. Our prayer is that you make it a priority to find your impulse in all these nasty tyrannical moments; plant seeds with your presence in the shit that you witness; remain united with the true value of your ideas and your ideals, and turn your heart toward your extraordinary story with you as the hero. Tag -- you're it -- go answer the call.

Tipping, leverage and sublimation points along with pendulum swings are all actions of unusual physical moments, when the norm is abolished and uniqueness occurs. These moments have an individual nature in the overall collection of nature . . . it makes their actions less predictable . . . they verge on the dimensions of magic over logic. There's little relationship with the standard linear forms of cause and effect. These are the solvents when dealing with intolerable circumstances such as tyrants and sociopathic rulers. Such was the magic that Mahatma Gandhi used in his strategic non-violent campaign to bring down the tyrannical rule of the British over India. The British had zero connection to the consequences of their actions and the Indians had zero power to defend themselves at any level. Gandhi employed the tipping; leverage; sublimation points, and pendulums of physics to bring down the rulers of the mightiest empire this world has experienced on a human level. With no awareness of the consequences of their actions, there's a brutal quality to the world that tyrants create. Strategic non-violence is a tool more powerful than their tyrannical violence, for it ultimately works on the level of collective consciousness, inspiration, faith and enthusiasm that can mobilize the masses beyond their own will. The unwilling become compelled to join these actions working at deeper levels of the psyche than the intellect, or intelligence can reach. This is when the world of tyrannical violence meets the universe of collective non-violence . . . there's no match . . . might succumbs to right . . . it's a unique law of physics. This is how evolution has survived for billions of years . . . ultimately the pendulum swings; the tipping point tips; the leverage lifts, and the sublimation unfolds. This is the unyielding power of faith, dedication, and nonviolence . . . this is your world right now and into the near future, for the tyrants are in the house. Our prayer is that you're ready for this moment; willing to take your place in history; able to ride the wave that delivers these tyrants to the laws beyond their laws, and remake this place with grace.

Today it's time to get real -- to 'real-ize' that cooperation and coordination are the only pathways to survival . . . every great species that has lived beyond a million years knows this. This is the juncture human beings now face. Everything is made up of light, and light travels at the speed of time until it's observed by the psyche. Once observed, light become images in a memory that doesn't change while time moves on at light-speed. This is a huge challenge for the psyche -- it stores so much memory in this static form, but the time of life continues at the speed of light . . . memories stagnate and lose light as they refuse to keep up with the times. For the past one hundred thousand years, the human capacity for memory storage has been increasing exponentially, but the ability to maintain light in this memory is failing and the human emotional body is becoming more valued than the physical one. Most human worlds are composed of these fixated feelings and emotional events -- held in memories becoming darker -- posing as personas, personalities, and realities. Most of this is not traveling with time at the speed of anything, but is stuck in a complete lack of emotional awareness or flexibility. Emotional education is an essential subject for schools right now as the human world shifts from reality to fantasy . . . as the truth becomes what you can convince people of. Emotional education is needed to produce tolerance in children destined to grow up in a world filled with people who are vastly different. As air travel accelerates migration, differences among neighbors are the norm . . . openness is required to survive. Changing with light is the nature of growth, while those obsessed with old rules and tradition are cemented in memories rapidly becoming dark. Such is the root cause of bigotry and phobias . . . all of which arise from static memory held in moments that aren't advancing with the light of time. Our prayer is that you train the children of this rapidly shifting world in the ways of their light body; that you enable this experience of life -- at the speed of light -- to replace the darkness of memory . . . allow life to get real and be light once again.

*B*iology is survival -- until your consciousness is able to compensate for this instinctual relationship with time -- the world of you, in the world you live in, is going to only be about you. To be inclusive of the needs of others, in the way that compassion requests, is an attribute that's learned through millions of years of trial and error. Most creatures have already gone through this evolutionary stage, but humans are young -- a recent phenomenon by the measure of all-time . . . not responding with this skill quite yet. This compassion is magical -- where sheer survival is quite logical. Those who are compassionate, conscious and magical are the new evolution. It's even displayed at the basic level of reproduction. The male delivers sperm -- which is obvious, predictable and very logical. The female controls permission to embrace the process of conception, gestation and an ability to deliver . . . not obvious; quite unpredictable, extremely magical, and clearly beyond male logic. Evolved, conscious and compassionate masculinity -- in nearly every creature on Earth -- serves this unfamiliar process from the position of respect, while honoring the deeper progression of magic. Unevolved and primitive masculinity wants to control this magic, turn it into logic, and use the powers of predictability to govern it. Because this is not possible, the primitive human male reverts to shame, blame and sexual competitions that entertain its erections, while retaining dominance through logic. He creates opinion pageants that have nothing to do with actual beauty . . . except in a false name and its faux crowns. This is the stage where unevolved humanity sits in this present moment -- a stage where primitive unconsciousness retains the power of 'en-force-ment' with masculine logic -- while evolving consciousness desires to retire this primitive ignorance, and honor the true value and significance of the feminine. Our prayer is that you recognize this moment human life has arrived at; that you open your heart to the progress taking place; that you realize yin and yang are forever equal . . . the GODDESS is quite different, yet equal to GOD.

Women are cosmically, emotionally, psychologically, and biologically more powerful than men. Yogi Bhajan referred to women as 'eagles', while the patriarchy -- slighting the feminine power -- referred to them as "chicks". Survival was a physical event for millions of years . . . masculine rule was natural, until it wasn't . . . and now it's not. In reaction, the masculine power-channels have devolved into creepy . . . nationally; internationally; religiously, and culturally creepy. The equal and opposite reaction is unfolding. Women -- and conscious men supporting this power -- are voicing and standing for the right to get real. Ignorance is something that's to be ignored no more, it must be challenged and changed at its immature core. Ignorance is now in the format of "baby boys" -- many in the bodies of "adult-ish men" -- clinging to a survival fantasy from the ancient past. So fitting for it to be taking place at the feet of strong women, for this is the exact nature of giving birth . . . this moment is giving birth to a future that's more real. As ignorance dies its difficult and anguished death, the old masculine-guard -- holding power that was never powerful, but a fear-based attitude of ancient-echoes rattling through fictionalized history -- resists the inevitable. Like the discovery and use of electricity -- the electricity was around forever, but it took time to understand the usefulness -- the Divine feminine power is the new lightbulb. In order to give birth to this reality, a reality that's as old as time, there's a polarity of ridiculous male characters sitting atop the world stage, all attempting to stand in its way. This is just the way such staging in nature is done, and these male figures are the caricatures of a dying meme, and as such, they appear more insane than ever. Our prayer is that you take your place in line with nature as this natural unfolding unfolds; that you embrace this moment as the birthing of everything to come . . . Goddesses taking their place with the Gods . . . reality taking the place of illusion . . . love replacing fits of male anger . . . and a new normal replacing crazy . . . the new normal of power that's calm.

*U*niversal health care; a comprehensive welfare system; the importance of everyone's education . . . all attitudes found in the great forests on Earth. In other words, the great forests know better . . . they've survived for three hundred and seventy million years because they care for each other and the Earth. The health of the forests demonstrate the collective health of life, and the Earth influences life in ways that science isn't capable of measuring yet. Everything about the Earth influences life, and this is why it's vital to respect all of the Earth's signs and signals. When the Earth quake's -- often at a depth below twenty miles -- the ground is responding like liquid; this affects the liquids in every life on Earth . . . seventy percent of every 'body'. Fracking -- which obvious to those who are awake increases quaking -- is adverse to life. The Earth's gravity translates into life's moods; the Earth's electromagnetics translate into signals in the brain; the sound of the Earth -- the Schumann resonance -- is essential to the attitudes throughout all kingdoms . . . minerals, plants and animals. Higher consciousness realizes this oneness, but ignorance and idiocy can't connect the connections. This is why you're here, for just beyond this current idiocy and arrogance is a human calm at the exact center of the ignorant storm. This calm delivers solid knowledge and wisdom of forever . . . forever is the soul's domain. Relating in forever terms, relates from the soul; you catch glimpses of the sheer vastness of the physics in creation. Here, in the calm of this universal wisdom, you connect with every other reachable and teachable incarnation. These are your soul's allies in this moment across the multiversal space.

Now is the gathering of these souls on Earth -- the new "crystal" touchstones sent to capture solutions . . . all the new "Christ". You are this new coming -- there have been countless before, and be countless after you, but right now, you're the ones. Our prayer is that you're good with this; that you welcome the responsibility, and recognize this moment without needing further signs . . . just accept it . . . do your part . . . enable life to thrive.

You are the new 'Coming' -- you're the enlightened one, not the only one, but one of the ones. You're the new 'Coming' in response to what's going on . . . it's happened many times before in countless moments throughout the history of endless planets all warranting huge responses to a desperate moment. Now is clearly one such moment, and here you are. There's a massive tear in the fabric of life, and within such a 'hole' are the clues to its resolution . . . you're one of the ones with the senses to know the resolutions that will challenge these challenges. This is a day, like nearly every other day, it's a starting point for the rest of all days. A hole in spacetime's fabric is a massive depression that's generally to be avoided, but this one's different . . . you're different . . . now it's time to explore this hole, and explore the whole of the hole. You see, there wasn't actually a 'big bang', there was a 'big stretch'. When a super-sun -- spinning just beyond the fabric of spacetime -- came close enough to the surface of the megaversal potential, it began stretching the surface inward under the greatest possible gravity with tension, pressure, stress, and friction. This surface conformed into a universe, and there are many such confirmations throughout all the Megaverses throughout the Multiverse. Countless universes stretching across the existence of forever, and these have been your training grounds, in between now and then. Unlike the masses who are tumbling into the present hole, you're different, more aware of the endless beginnings . . . aware that there's always something before and after . . . refusing to believe in the fantasy of limits . . . determined to know the solutions to now. This is why you're the new 'Coming' -- the crystal clarity. Our prayer is that you'll take what happens today as your signal to ignite magic without limits; the signal that enforces what you've come here to be; that you have no restraints as life plunges into this hole in the fabric. Catch the ones who are reachable and teachable in your magical net . . . these ones will join you in the new 'Coming'. No matter what else happens today, it's just the first day of forever.

Everyone is made up of countless characters . . . mastery is when all these characters are pointed and pulling in the same direction. On a masterful journey from infinity to your identity, you'll meet -- without meeting -- one character who's being without doing, who breathes in you without being the breather, in a web that has no weaver . . . this is the character known as your 'Master' . . . your infinite stranger . . . the person who's authentically 'you' inside of you. This is the genius in everyone, and the level of your conscious awareness will either allow this genius to be exposed, or remain hidden. This is the master-character, and the level of your mastery is determined by the level of this character's involvement. This is the character containing your powers of intuition and commitment. When you're wanting, claiming, and struggling to achieve -- even if only for yourself -- neither the genius, nor the infinite stranger have any role in your world. In order to engage and sustain a relationship with this masterful character, your life must be attached to a mission, or a vision of your larger purpose. Once this is your constant model, you'll ride the momentum of this character with ease. As you ride this momentum, it's important to be conscious of your breathing without taking credit as the breather . . . without taking the credit, you experience no debt or doubt. This is known as humble, but it's actually more than humility . . . it's a state of total surrender to being, and the boundary between doing and being is difficult to travel. It's knowing that everything is being done with your hands and mind, while not being the doer. A meditation to work with this power is consciously breathing without being the breather.

This is the domain of your infinite stranger; the one who's actually breathing life into your life; the one who supports your masterful genius. Our prayer is that you sit with this meditation for the months of daily practice required to perfect it. This is one of many keys to your Master's realm connecting infinity to your identity . . . experience this with commitment . . . enjoy the super-intuition and genius that is you.

You're a miracle of nature with endless solutions . . . you stand out. When life breaks natural laws and disrupts the nature of universal forces -- dimensions disintegrate to introduce higher ones . . . ones filled with impossibilities and miracles when viewed from current beliefs. This repeats many times through astronomical history, and with this comes astro-migrations . . . highly advanced souls migrating from one universe to another, from one megaverse to another. This is who you are -- an alien sent to Earth to break up human laws that are breaking the natural laws of universal forces. Spaceship "Aliens" shown in stone documents of Samaria and other places on Earth, are less advanced. You're the ones that've migrated in 'soul-bodies' to incarnate in physical bodies here on Earth. You're a 'non-law-gical' -- more 'ma-gical' being, living beyond the laws of man to follow the laws of nature . . . a true "illegal alien". You've come to this world to save this world . . . "illegal aliens" working against the forces of logic (law-gic) in order to bring about balance. You're a reaction, not from this Earth, or this galaxy, or even this Universe . . . your from far beyond the curve of the horizon where advances are trillions, even quadrillions of years beyond Earth. You're here to fill the holes in logic; to save life from crashing through these 'holes' of unnatural results from their assemblage of the tangents from tangents . . . of life in 'tragical' terms. You're here to contribute 'magical' solutions, but lower dimensions don't believe in this magic except when performed by a single more "special" being to be worshipped . . . not attainable by the normal ones. Face it -- you're not normal -- and now's the time to be that savior. Just like the stories of ones from the past only this time it's different . . . there are millions of you around the Earth . . . it's time to join hands. You've all been sent from the advanced worlds to save this struggling one. Our prayer is that you're willing to stand out in order to be outstanding; that you take on the 'beyond normal' job you were sent here to fulfill . . . to be that illegal alien . . . to be the miracle solutions.

*L*ife stood up seven million years ago -- added the third dimension for the perception of depth in its full character, and has spent seven eons exploring this. One hundred and twenty-five thousand years ago, once the brain had expanded to hold memory, life added the fourth dimension of sequential time. The next 'standing up' is raising the Kundalini to more conscious levels of human awareness. The third dimension exhausted its application when humans began controlling land rather than sharing its purpose of land for life. The fourth dimension (time) has now exhausted its application . . . humans have begun buying and selling it rather than embracing it's wealth. With each of these advancing dimensions there's tremendous struggle within and without, when the older exhausted dimension opens a doorway out of necessity, to the next dimension. The fifth dimension is where all time is one moment -- past, present, and future as one. With such a shift, money -- instead of transacting time -- will explore the full richness of its value. The old transactions of fixation on reasons, will be forced into new standards of greater trust without reasons. This produces tremendous anxiety amongst those fixated on the old standards of "time is money". It's progressing at this very moment . . . a crisis of time . . . a reduction of space . . . the ultimate transformation of dimensions. Destruction of rainforests, public lands, waters, and air -- coupled with the reduction of time from the manipulation of money's search for cheaper resources -- is a meaningless stretch into less. These are indicators that a new dimension is birthing. The second dimension introduced trial and error into evolution; the third dimension introduced migration;

the fourth dimension introduced memory and the mind . . . the fifth dimension will introduce the constant use of trust without a measuring tool . . . the completion of total surrender. Our prayer is that you're ready, willing, and able to walk through this door of dimension into mastery; that you take hold of it like you own it, and share it like it belongs to everyone, for this is a moment that will not wait . . . the moment you've been waiting for.

Intuitive faith and trust is knowing without reason . . . an unreasonable knowing. This is the heart centered brain and the brain of the gut . . . the hunch in your gut and the hint in your heart. On the other side of you, there's your intelligent concern, the doubt that asks for reasons. This is not a bad thing -- it comes from your head brain which has perfect two dimensional value, but it can't be the exclusive judge if you want success to be fulfillment. Because you've evolved through countless incarnations of survival crisis, you've come to rely upon intelligent concern and doubt in order to arrive where you are at this time, but it won't take you to where you're going. It's said in the ancient teachings there's a place for both, and there's a must for both . . . intelligent concern with reasonable doubting, must be accompanied by an intuitive faith and trust of unreasonable knowing. This is the balance of a trilogy of perspectives, the head brain's two dimensions, with the heart brain and gut brain's other-dimensions. This balance point is a doorway to the master within you . . . the master that's aware of everything, it's inside of each and every person. But your 'will' gets in the way, just like in breathing -- you think you're breathing -- but you're not breathing, you're being breathed. When you get in touch with the master that's breathing you, you're in touch with the master that's being you. The great spiritualists always said, "If you're not being you, there is no you . . . there's an imposter pretending to be you. That imposter is a painful existence, and it's that painful existence that's subsidized by all of this world's frantic chase to purchase pleasure. This is what humanity is constantly slaving for. But when you let that inner master to be masterful, you're a witness to the most outstanding performance ever. Our prayer is that you come to the balance of unreasonable knowing alongside your intelligent concern; that you connect with your head, heart and gut whenever you're connecting with anyone or anything, and when the door to the master within you opens, you walk through and make yourself at home . . . like you own it.

The 'what is wrong' and the 'what is right' are of equal quantity and quality in every point of space -- every moment of time. It's compelling to focus on what's wrong -- this has always been 'severely' coupled to the survival of moments. The negative mind -- trained by these high stakes survival strategies and tactics -- is currently organized by 'cautious money' to hesitate in the presence of inspiration -- always look for the pitfalls even when inspired -- don't be a fool -- it can't be that magical -- stick with your logical mind even when it decreases the inspiration. This is marketed as being intelligent -- "it's why business works" -- if you're not working this way, you're not being smart. It creates a compelling high stress in its presence, and to move away from this feels irresponsible, yet the entire time you're focused on what's wrong, biologically this is all you can see. As you work to reduce the momentum of 'what's wrong', your psycho-emotional system increases the imagery of urgency to maintain the momentum . . . "don't be fooled," the emotions warn. There's a biological algorithm that's rarely used, but far more inspiring . . . and more effective too. The simple explanation of this unique human program: you can increase the 'what is right' more rapidly than you can decrease the 'what is wrong' . . . ultimately they give the same result of solution, but there's an entirely different experience in the process. This alternative flies in the face of pressure being the best stimulant; of stress being a working positive; of friction leading to positive outcomes, and all those fear-based business, survival-oriented attitudes . . . collected over millions of survival years. This alternative orientation relies on: when the heart-brain is wide open -- the polarities demonstrate the path of inclination where inspiration supersedes desperation. Our prayer is that you shift to this algorithm; allow your inspiration to run your projects in this way; focus on the 'what's right' and don't fear being the fool; teach the world by the example of your "intuitive" faith, not the skillsets attached to your "intelligent" concerns.

Wisdom says: a debate without rebuttal demonstrates the obvious . . . when clarity is obvious, and there's still debate, the debate is out of ignorance. Ignorance isn't the absence of awareness, it's ignoring it. Caring for others is a current debate of ignorance. The higher the consciousness of a species, the more it cares for the wellbeing of other members. Allowing for anything to take precedence over wellbeing of life is to ignore the value of life. There are measures of what's always been known as 'commons' -- what is common to the wellbeing and best interest of life itself. Health-care and healing are compassionate gestures of one life to another life -- this qualifies it to be of common interest to life. All examples of life-forms lasting through extensive epochs of time are dominated by the individuals caring for each other as deeply as the individuals have cared for themselves. This produces a sustainable system that permeates environments -- not just neighborhoods. No life-form, anywhere on planet Earth, has "castles" for some members and ghettos for others. This is uniquely human and is an unsustainable/unevolved model. Universal models create equilibrium and stability; such models are higher and more advanced by every evolutionary standard. Any form of life that adapts universal care, finds the ultimate sustainability. This has enabled the forests of the world to survive for three hundred and seventy million years . . . one hundred times longer than humans and pre-human ancestors have lived. Forests don't create factions, nor compete for territory; they have a fully formed value based banking systems . . . no debt; they have childcare; welfare and zero warfare . . . all formulas of universally available longevity. Life-cultures without these longevity based systems are the 'weak-links' in the chain of evolution. This is not ill intent, but a byproduct of zero intent, and zero intent is an infancy without maturity . . . an unsupervised house. Our prayer is that you're an adult in this one-room schoolhouse Earth; that you promote universal care for longevity-based, sustainable environments and realize this is not a debate . . . this is a higher path.

*G*raphene is a single (one atom thick) layer of hexagonally bonded carbon atoms. Researchers have analyzed graphene and found that this matter -- only five per cent the density of steel -- is ten times stronger than steel. They've also found, you can replace the carbon material with anything, it's the geometry of the bond that's the real determining factor. This research is demonstrating, if you introduce a particular geometry into any moment -- no matter how vague a substance might be -- you can produce a strong physical reality. This is science proving the deepest visions of the great masters, prophets and avatars, who've all said: "Everything comes from sound." Imagine the scriptures describing the origins of creation, "In the beginning was the word." They are actually saying that in the beginning was a sound . . . just a sound plus [some] 'particular' geometry created everything. Think of your wildest dreams and your fondest ideas . . . since matter is 'anything' plus a sacred geometry . . . perhaps this geometry can manifest the sounds of your ideas. This is what the masters, prophets and avatars all claimed throughout time. This is the alchemy they've described as pure physics and chemistry . . . the truer version of infinite prosperity . . . the unending abundance that's always there. They've also said that the ways to create these geometries -- to manifest anything out of nothing -- is to believe; to discipline yourself into holding faith and trust, and do this right alongside your ideas, dreams, and hopes. Geometry is a solution like an 'other-dimensional' form of water . . . built from ultra-faith; profound trust, and endless compassion. These teachings of the masters also say that the thoughts and actions, not holding these sacred geometries of faith, trust and compassion, are working against your ability for miracles. Earth needs your miracles right now. Our prayer is that you realize you're a miracle worker; that you discipline some time each day to develop this power; that you take your great ideas and work to manifest their rewards . . . like a freeze-dried miracle . . . just add water . . . you're the solution.

*T*homas Edison once said, "There are no rules here -- we're trying to accomplish something." That's the heart, inspiration, determination and spirit of an inventor speaking. You're an inventor . . . the inventor of your next breath -- your next moment -- ones that have never existed, and never will again. What are you 'free' to accomplish with these moments? The real answer . . . anything you can imagine. Rules are the limiting logic of two dimensional attempts to guarantee safety and avoid conflict, but they can also stifle innovation. Innovation and safety don't always coexist. Stress will oppose invention to prove the value of rules over the spirit of innovation. Such is the nature of many disciplines that stress the rules over having an experience. Such is the nature of many institutions that have lost touch with their innovative beginnings, like nations, religions, cultures, and ideas. The idea of human societies, and everything that comes with it -- including politics and religions -- are extensions of the innovation of 'campfires'. Gatherings took place around these campfires to provide warmth and security; to cook food and extend comfort to the individuals. Gathering together was more efficient than going it alone and rules began as a means of maintaining the purpose of the warmth, security, food and comfort. But rules -- once established -- are not innovative, and innovation must then reach through the rules -- take a moment out beyond the rules -- dare to ask the questions that reconsider the value of the rules. If the value no longer exists, then it's time to shift the rules. Your life was created to invent and innovate the future, not blindly follow the rules from the past. Our prayer is that you're courageous enough to relax the rules; that you're not here to attack the rules, but you're also not attached to them; that you're prepared to compassionately respond to those who question your authority to innovate; that you're willing to stand alone -- away from the comfort of the community campfire if necessary -- to innovate a future that produces an invention to serve everyone's needs . . . not just the rule's needs.

*H*uman intelligence: the Brain's electromagnetic and chemical relays, synchronized with resonance signals -- the frequency of the Earth -- perceiving through the senses to define life with psycho-emotional markers. It's the vast diversity that excites the senses to the beauty of nature and creation . . . the diversity inspires you. But when people look for the beauty in other people, it's not the diversity, but the predictability that senses safety, and this safety then allows for the sense of love. These moments take place because in addition to the space you occupy, you also have the measure of time. Time is produced when soul enters the body through the lens of ego. Throughout life, the ego will either work with your highest denominator of consciousness, or ignore it. When it ignores this, the physical body becomes the primary reference point. The physical body is mortal, and it knows this, so time seems limited and in short supply. The ego then looks for safety in the limitations, rather than abundance in the infinite diversity that's everywhere. When the sensation of time is not limited, but is infinite, it produces moments of space that appear in your senses to contain all you require or desire . . . right there . . . always. This is the relation of ego and consciousness and the difference is in the angles that consciousness supplies to your point of view. When the vast majority of humanity are under-evolved and ignoring the higher denominators of consciousness, then both time and space will seem limited. Under this influence -- the ego attaches to the lower denominators -- the sense of lack dominates and hoarding proliferates; money becomes the goal, not the trust; logic becomes the governing factor, not a balance to the miracles;

predictability reigns supreme, and the grandeur of nature and everything natural become unimportantly at risk as human intelligence becomes unintelligent and falls out of synchronicity with the frequency of the Earth. This is where the world is at today. Our prayer is that you know you have an answer, and you activate this answer every day with the lens of your ego . . . make this the time for your life.

The twenty-first century is a re-evolution; a revolution of issues that've plagued Earth the past twenty-five thousand years. These are the two dimensional views consuming humans in a multidimensional world . . . the two dimensions of right vs wrong; good vs bad; men vs women; this way vs that way -- rather than always being compatible. In order to change this broken pattern, you've been born to break it. You're the radical disruptors -- sent to this planet in the Universe at this moment in time, to alter the course of history and save all life on Earth. You're one of those with this responsibility and now is the time to live it . . . completely stretched into your character, knowing everything that you ever want or need will always be there for you. Living at such a level of trust and faith is new for most, but not for you. You've been practicing this for lifetimes on planets far more advanced than you now even imagine. Except for those very few, throughout history, who've been documented as reaching such a state of nirvana, no one really knows what you're all about. The key to sustaining your state of realization in all this doubt, is to honor the boundaries that don't exist . . . not non-existent because no one believes in them, but non-existent because they're actually not there. This was the lecture Lord Krishna gave Arjuna in the Bhagavad Gita; this is the time for the discipline of knowing the emotions, feelings and drives of your lower self, and redirecting them in this world. With these emotions and feelings not redirected, those reaching this level will avoid the unevolved people, go into seclusion and hide your talents. This is not those times; this is not why you're here on Earth, there's a need for your highest consciousness to immerse itself into the societies of this world. This revolution is 'Grishtha Ashram' as explained by Guru Nanak . . . the life of an enlightened householder . . . not a renunciate. Our prayer is that you flush the doubts that hold a two dimensional view of this multi-dimensional time; that you redirect your base emotions of fear and doubt to guide you -- not stop you. Keep-up and you'll be miraculously kept up.

*M*icromorphosis is when life -- sometimes just in parts -- produces massive evolutionary changes through tiny unnoticeable ways. It takes time for these tipping-point changes to unfold, but nature focuses on success and survival. Successful nature is an art as well as a science, and the outcome -- when art is involved -- is stimulated by opinions. Like convincing the world that realities are truths, people must release old rigid habits of "reality" . . . Galileo discovered this in a huge way. Here's a habit that would be critical to change: living for the truth, not dying for it -- this would eliminate the patriarchy; retire the false fervor of patriotism, and ultimately erase the intensity of territorial boundaries that have led to wars, widespread famine, poverty, and inhuman cruelty. What a gift it would be to set humanity free to roam on an ecologically robust planet of abundance. To do this however, you must fully commit to unconditionally trusting, being radically disruptive, and walking as if consciousness just got sober, a sobriety of knowing you must convert the deeply unconscious into this higher awareness. It's not going to happen . . . it's time for an alternative approach. The Bible warns of this futility -- it says, "Don't cast pearls before swine." But this verse supports the mutilation of oysters, and a false supposition that pigs aren't intelligent. What if you just realized: you can't teach trigonometry, or any higher subject, to a four year old, and the vast majority of humans -- definitely the ruling class -- are scared children. Their two dimensional thinking limits flexibility. Fixated on good 'v' bad, right 'v' wrong, friend 'v' foe, and safe 'v' fear -- eliminates stretching their third dimensional space through any amount of fourth dimension time . . . you need a 'work-around'. Our prayer is that you master the work-around; deflect the 'adult-child's' attitudes for the moment and concentrate on preaching to the choir . . . most of them are still sleeping, not yet singing. Wake up the choir to a conscious sobriety and produce a tipping-point of micromorphosis . . . little moves producing huge changes.

In the distance of spacetime -- far - far from the big bang, the big squeeze, or the big leap of faith -- if you see it that way -- there's an image of how it never ever began, because it really couldn't have. This is the quantum quality of omniscience, where the soul is more relevant than the body, and the body is extremely relevant. Religions have been inspired, over the ages, to make up stories of how this might all work. Using a casts of characters, and hierarchies much like here on Earth, they've promoted these stories that are quite irrelevant to the cosmos, for the cosmos is not about characters, or stories, and definitely not about hierarchies. However, these characters and their stories do provide a sense of safety for the children, but then the adults tend to use them for power and advantage where there is none. 'Infinity/eternity' is astronomical, and these stories are inaccurate, other than as inspiration. To make you feel safe, their characters try to make it all familiar and small by measuring that which is beyond measure. However, just as beauty is in the eyes of the beholder . . . safety is also. You can alter your sense of beautiful, you can also alter your sense of what's safe, and when you feel safe, your entire system opens to what those religious prophets experienced . . . the 'ocean' that holds, supports and nourishes everything. Always present, whether you experience it or not, it's known to the ancients as Narayan, the ocean of all the angles of solutions, with love, joy, bliss and peace. Every religion created their stories to depict this safety. In your own story, whenever you feel safe, and you feel this love, joy and peace -- if someone else is present, you'll "blame" them and say, "I love you". But you're not actually loving them, you're experiencing the love that's always there . . . everywhere. You've simply taken a leap of faith into safety. Our prayer is that you take these leaps often; that you experience infinity as the love, joy and peace that's everywhere, and then "blame" it on as many people as you can. Spread the love that goes around and it will definitely come back around by saying "love you" . . . even to strangers.

In the year 1900, there were one and a half billion people on the Earth, and eighty-five percent of all money on Earth was circulating in the streets to purchase food, clothing, shelter and transportation for life. Today, there are seven and a half billion people on Earth, and seventy-five percent of all money on Earth never touches the streets. It's suspended in what's called the 'rambling hoard' . . . a system of hoarding and investing for the sake of trading money to make money. It's literally been taken out of circulating for everyone's life, and is suspended in a hoard for the purpose of the false security in a few lives. Masters throughout the ages have taught humanity to learn from the heart. The heart exerts in order to give and then completely relaxes in order to receive back. This is a cycle that keeps the circulatory system -- which is central and vital to life -- healthy, successful and fulfilling. When circulation does not completely relax to receive, pressure builds and eventually the body suffers from hypertension. Under this increased pressure, the blood begins abnormally clotting, and the body breaks down in a variety of disorders. Abnormal "clotting" is the current epidemic of hoarding, where an uneven amount of money is being held by an unequal amount of life . . . the system is due for a "stroke" or central heart "attack". When a person does not relax to receive, but creates tension to get, they never experience the joy of receiving . . . they're compelled to do more to get more and this produces even greater tension. An endless cycle of striving, doing and getting never experiences the joy of receiving . . . hoarding and amassing ever larger, unsatisfying quantities of capital is the result. This is the root cause of poverty, and the heart of compassion is at risk of failing under this pressure of greed . . . the clots of capital are causing strokes in the system. Our prayer is that you're an active medicine for the solution; that you're vigorously relaxed around the positive circulation of capital, and doing your part -- no matter how small -- to relieve the pressure by sharing and caring for a global solution . . . poverty is not humane.

*E*go is the glue that holds soul in body . . . a passive servant that performs what you charge it to do. Ego has a bad reputation, but the bad reputation comes from thousands of years of selfish, survival oriented, exclusive behavior. The great masters would cultivate the ego for greater service, the competitive masters would put ego down as a bad thing in order to gain an advantage over the students. With a strong and powerful ego, pointed in a benevolent and compassionate direction of serving life and humanity, you have the opportunity to make a huge difference . . . the opportunity to create change that's meaningful to every life. To use ego as a benevolent tool; a compassionate tool; a radically disruptive tool, the masters developed the mantra 'Ha'. A sound that brings the energy from the base of your spine up to the heart center. It's both the sound of laughing and crying. When it's laughing, your energy comes from the base up to the heart, saying I have something to share. When it's crying, your energy comes from the base to the heart, saying I need help . . . both are an act of the ego . . . one is giving and one is needing. When you add a trilled 'r' to the end of the 'Ha' it becomes 'Har'. The 'r' uses the tongue and connected fascia to move this energy from the heart through the mouth to the crown. The mantra 'Har' is a statement from the base of your being to your crown. It enables your ego to be used for the benefit of all, while it's saying you're both laughing and crying . . . you have something to share and you also need help. This is life at its core; this is life projected so that everyone knows the needs of each other and are "banking" on those needs being cared for and shared from. This is the future of banking and the proper use of economics; this is humanity being humane, and this is the only way life will ultimately profit. Our prayer is that you take the root of this mantra as the core of your ego and sign on to the new economics; use your humane ability to share and care -- guide the purpose and meaning of your life to create an exchange of trust on Earth . . . an economics that supports all life . . . a truly conscious form of capital.

*A*nomalous phenomena -- a snowflake -- the individuation of you -- with all the deviations from anything common. Everyone is original . . . an exact copy of absolutely nothing . . . the very first of everything with no similarities to anything. Emotional pain arises when you attempt to fit in and be just like others . . . liking to hide the anomaly that's you. You're the very first and there will never be another . . . this is the nature of each incarnation. Your task is to be the most anomalous of the phenomenon of you. There has never been another person exactly like this version of you; there is no other person exactly like this version of you; there will never be a version of any person that's exactly like this current version of you -- so if you are not being exactly like you -- then when you die -- the 'you-in-you' never existed. You have every authority to be you and this authority is immortal. For you to follow the rules is a convenience, but to do it with immortally you must follow them creatively . . . not exactly. This is not to be unethical, or immoral, this is to be you and to compassionately question everything. Like, who made up the original rules that make up the current rules? And, who found the authority to obfuscate your authority . . . to confuse and obscure the power of your being. Who has the right to question the configurations of a global map based on antiquated wars that stops human migration -- when the birds, four legged creatures, fish and even the insects are free to roam on the land, seas, and skies . . . to go anywhere they please? Beauty is another rule that you must question, for it's purely an opinion held within the senses of some anonymous witness . . . an opinion that's been captured and defined, but in fact beauty is available everywhere in everything . . . it's in your eyes. This is the new mastery -- the new sages, gurus, and prophets . . . this is the new revelation. Our prayer is that you embrace the modern moment; resist the old traditional attitudes that believe change is incorrect . . . move with the times and unfold the unlimited you . . . prosper in this rapidly growing universal phenomenon . . . you be you.

Intuition is the discovery of the unemotional and unimaginable amongst the emotions and feelings that want to control the waves of chaotic human attitudes. It's the noiselessness amongst the noise . . . the deep silence that's always calm, accurate and present no matter how chaotic the levels on the surface are. This is the uncertainty of the unimaginable' nature that never competes in the realms of certainty. It's always there, and when certainty breaks down, the unimaginable begins to take over. When the unimaginable starts taking over, discovery becomes more common. Then when discovery becomes quite common, you relax within your innocence, because you're not needing to be certain, and you're also not needing to be afraid. This is when answers and solutions come pouring through your intuition . . . they've always been there, right alongside the challenges and the questions and the emotions. The exact solutions to everything you're facing in this world today are available -- but they're not within the public arguments . . . not on the surface of the public conversations filled with emotions and opinions of certainty. They're to be found outside these arguments and debates; they're waiting to be discovered without proof that they'll work, or are even worthy of consideration . . . but you'll know them when they appear. And when you first discover them they'll have no convincing details . . . they'll be discounted quickly and you'll not be able to defend them. They require faith for activation -- this is the nature of the unimaginable. Real solutions are unimaginable and every day you must give yourself an opportunity to go where the 'unimaginables' exist . . . every day you must dream. Our prayer is that you allow yourself this dream time each day; save up the world's greatest challenges to be solved in unimaginable ways; allow these solutions to freely speak for themselves. Listen carefully, don't interrupt the silence. Everything of value comes from this engine of creation that's still working and is now needed more than ever. You can save the world -- not by yourself -- but start by becoming outrageously intuitive and all the help you require will show up.

*F*eelings are composite drawings of times within times that have been accumulated over the genetic lineage of a family's generational history. They're not accurate measures of what's actually taking place in the present, because they've so much that's invested from the past. But as defense mechanisms they'll organize a brute response to the moment in order to survive the moment. This is why a crowd will follow a bully, or a bullying type of attitude. These are survival instincts that've been carried from the ancient past through strains of surviving DNA. They have great abilities to survive, but very little refinement that applies understanding to the current moment. Remember this when you're deeply disappointed; have hurt feelings, or feel betrayed . . . this will be survived, but not solved with a reaction. In order to solve these feelings you'll need to dive deeper, contemplate and meditate from a neutral position; remove yourself as the subject and the object of the feelings, and contemplate the pain without being personally hurt. The situation will begin to speak to you . . . begin to speak for itself. Ultimately -- even when all sides believe there's something really wrong -- the source of the dilemma will reveal itself far beyond this perceived space and time. The "wrong" is simply demonstrating a target -- one that's easy to blame -- but the blame is an echo of an echo, from another blame, from another time of a time beyond time. Reaction is a two-dimensional expression . . . right-wrong . . . good-bad, but solutions are not two dimensional. They never exist within the same dimension as the problem. Only revenge redefined as "justice" lives alongside the feelings of hurt . . . solutions live in a higher perspective.

Our prayer is that you take the time to invest in solutions; allow them to weave through this pathway of feelings; remove the rush and you'll remove the blocks; sit neutrally with pure feelings, and follow the sensations to their source. Here you'll discover what's actually being experienced. This is you being a master and teaching mastery by example. This is you making the world a better place one moment at a time.

In order for the universe to persist -- to exist beyond any moment leading to momentum and then to all those momentous opportunities -- it must be constantly in motion, in a continuous state of change, inherently unpredictable, and radically disruptive to any stasis. This is not logical and never controllable . . . it feels completely out of control. This is what's at the very core of cause, change, challenge, opportunity, and growth. It's the 'encoded' codes of persistence and the illogical disruption of existence. In order for this to take place, there's a moment at nearly every level of awareness in which the universe throws a complete fit that fits, but doesn't fit. This is what you're feeling right now if you're paying attention. You're experiencing this universal urge for nature to be natural, for the false idiocies to become actual, for reality to finally get real and to rage completely out of control. This is the urge that's stronger right now than ever, and if you're not experiencing this radical disruption, it's time to wake up. In the midst of this challenge and change -- while the more unconscious ones are reacting with violent attempts to control their phobias with bigotry -- the super-consciousness is moving to its most central point where all there is is love. This is universal synchronicity . . . love is the universal constant . . . an ocean of liquidity . . . the consistency of solutions . . . the insistency of answers. Known as Narayan to the ancient teachings, this love is not something that you can own, or give. It's something you experience, and it's always there whether you experience it or not . . . it's there forever. Our prayer is that you are who you are -- a radical disruptor; that you go where you grow without requiring it to be nice; that in this environment that doesn't fit, you throw a fit that doesn't work, and as a result you align with the consistency and insistency of growth . . . occupying the space that's not yet occupied, in order to enter a space -- in your 'self' -- that does not yet exist. This is a radical disruption the universe is inspiring right now, and if anything feels normal . . . you're asleep . . . wake up.

The year of 2017 is 2+0+1+7 = 10 . . . the master's number . . . the 'zero' of surrender following the 'one' that's in everything. 2017 is a year of mastery. It's said that mastery is being the exact same love on the inside, no matter what's happening on the outside . . . you're unaffected by changes, but experiencing them exactly as they are. Now you're able to respond to precisely what each moment needs. This is mastery -- it doesn't complain -- it never blames -- it doesn't treat anything, or anyone unfairly. This is the attitude that's essential in this era of massive change. Life is entering an evolutionary period of sublimation . . . a time in which the only constant will be change; the only common measure will be the uncommon differences, where humans stretch out of sameness and into their actual uniqueness. It's a period of self-expression replacing repression and depression. This is evolution reacting to stagnation with a radical disruption. But those in charge of humanity's laws and orders are not mastering life, they're becoming fearful of the changes -- they're becoming tight and rigid. As "leadership" devolves into the opposite of mastery, their world becomes a scary mystery; changes and differences are seen as threatening, and bigotry becomes the comfort blanket. Politicians are winning elections, all around the world, on platforms of bias against the constant variables; discrimination against the ever-present differences, and xenophobia as a right of self-preservation. When this is the "world", brute force is the religion, and guns are the sacrament. This is how all the great religions of this world -- founded by peaceful and enlightened masters -- have been turned into battle cries on every side. Our prayer, in this year of mastery, is that you master the dilemmas facing humanity; that you take the cards that're being dealt, and discover the winning hand is when every hand wins; where differences are honored not feared; where each person is valued for their unique contribution, and as changes occur on the outside, the love in your heart remains exactly the same. This is mastery, and the leader-shift this world is waiting for is you.

Time is a messenger that registers and measures . . . humans are aware of time, and whatever you're aware of, you can use. The use of time is both a blessing and a trap . . . a blessing when you own it as a divine synchronicity -- a trap when it bewilders you with a helpless sense that "stuff" just happens. Time is also a way for those who've gone before you -- of all kinds and specie -- to reconnect from a higher perspective . . . a doorway into other dimensions. There, just beyond the laws of two dimensional logic; beyond the geography of three dimensional space; beyond the moments of four dimensional time, there's a doorway that leads to realms of non-logical guidance. It can't be measured, or explained with reason, space or time. This is the realm of knowing without reasons (unreasonable knowing), of intuition without explanation, and a connection that surrounds everything. Often referred to as Angels, Fairies, Elves and Power-animals, this energy is everywhere in huge quantities . . . a number known in scriptures and sacred texts as the 'Legions'. Beyond logic and reason, this energy only waits for your authorization "code" to connect and protect. This code is your awareness and belief in the existence of this energy, no matter what form you picture it as. The present world is consumed with stricter logic, double blind studies, reasons, and an obsession with brute force. Concentrating on these attitudes it calls "reality", believing it's all in laws of logic, and a simplicity as order -- humans scurry about like small children nursing on predictability to feel "safe". "GOD" becomes this massive father figure . . . definable, predictable, describable and accountable. Atheists believe that they don't believe at all, but their simply rejecting -- like the Zen Buddhists do -- this overly simplistic description of infinite omnipresence. Every year is your opportunity to grow beyond such logic and become infinite 'Zero' while standing in the midst of everything as the 'One' thing. Our prayer is that every year measures the breakthroughs to your mastery . . . stand up and measure up . . . claim it and show up. Be the most powerful version of you.

This world -- by Carl Jung's definition -- is clinically insane. It does the same things over and over, expecting different responses. Every year the flu changes and needs a new vaccine. If you don't imagine the next opportunity, the possibility won't be available when it arrives. Allow your imagination to release you into this very moment, for an ideal world is an imagined world, and imagination requires time. Leonardo da Vinci imagined helicopters and submarines that required centuries and the imagination of others until submarines and helicopters became real. When imagination is maintained through all of the propositions and oppositions of time, it will ultimately and naturally manifest. This is true within any force, and with any idea. It was Einstein who said, "The imagination of today is a reality of tomorrow." Within every ideal world, there's an idea world. And because there's an ideal world in the future, that world will exist in today's imagined ideas . . . hold these long enough and they becomes actual. Ideals are made from your highest values, like humanity becoming humane; like peace existing on Earth. These values must be imagined in their highest forms, and held until they manifest. If armies could have ever solved the human dilemmas of injustice, they would've done so by now . . . armies have been around a very long time. And like doctor's responding to the flu -- there needs to be a new response for peace. Armies are responding to the flu of today, with vaccines from a thousand years ago. Law and order does not create either law, or order, and bombing for peace is very old thinking in a brand new world. Every master understands peace on every level is at the core of all matter. It's the ease, joy, knowing, and liberation that's always there. Armies and wars don't create it, they disrupt it. Our prayer is that you combine your imagination, intuition and creativity; allow your imagination to release you into this moment without holding on to the past; intuit what this moment brings, and apply creative responses to what that is -- not what it was. Imagine peace . . . hold this in your heart . . . intuition will show the way . . . you know it will.

Conscious humans must now take uncomfortable actions and become comfortable in the discomfort. Unconsciousness is destroying life by stealing the Earth's treasury of resources. The solutions aren't completely known, but now is the time to take the drastic actions that uncover them. Predicted by prophets throughout history; now is when innovative 'radical-disrupters' must implement dreams that make no immediate sense, but end up making the difference. You're an evolutionary reaction to devolution's departure from sustainability -- humanity has abandoned the heart center as its connection to time and to each other. This disastrous departure began in the North, tens of thousands of years ago with the advancing Ice Ages. Self-perpetuating psycho-emotional patterns continue to echo this terrifying time into the present and no one's to blame. Today's perpetrators of this eco-disaster are just the current lens through which these old terrors are being retained. Carnivores, territorial controls, pillaging, and 'intra-specie-violence' are the terrifying echoes from that ancient history. The fourth dimension of time is a gift of breathing life through the heart center . . . the heart still beats out the present moment, but no one's listening. Today's world is being destroyed by a slave's version of time measured with money. Two dimensions were corrupted by the dogmas of false theologies, the rights and wrongs that've made humans afraid to reach beyond their mortal limits. The third dimension of space was corrupted by the enclosure of land and ownership. Now the fourth dimension of time is being bought and sold . . . creating slaves of every-one, everywhere. It's time to open the fifth dimension -- accessed through dreams and meditations -- a theta-brain-state where creative solutions from higher dimensions solve problems that are here right now. Our prayer is that you sustain a daily practice to remain in this "dream-state" long enough to open these doors of higher perception; that you reach out on the beams of light-years and capture future solutions for this current moment . . . become a true master . . . discover who you truly are.

Thieves have captured three dimensional power, but there's dimensions beyond this which they've no recognition of, and are in denial of, that have far greater power. This is an advantage of consciousness, and now is the time to take advantage of this advantage. Make a New Year's resolution that you'll create a NEW way with NEW attitudes like, "God grant me the stubbornness to never accept that which I cannot change, but to reach beyond these three dimensions that appear impossible and discover hidden solutions with intuition." To not evolve, but to devolve is a dangerous inaction in these dangerous times. Devolution is now a threat to the life of many species . . . a threat to any life is a threat to all life. This is why the word devil is common to both words 'evil' and 'devolve'. Selfishness and timidity cause evil devolution in such critical times . . . a work of the thieves enabled by conscious inaction. We're entering a sublimation moment in human history where ignorance has become more powerful and troublesome, and the highly conscious are stuck in timid frustration. These are not the assigned roles, but the default roles within devolution's errors . . . the nature of selfish thieves and evil inactivity. This is a critical moment that's been predicted for thousands of years in ancient scriptures such as the Bhavishya Purana. Bhavishya means history of the future; Purana means verse . . . a writing of future times as if they've already taken place. One of these future histories predicts the widespread ignorance of today, with humanity in a transition from violent ignorance to conscious compassion. Ignorance is holding power and conscious compassion hasn't picked up the pace. This is the most delicate moment in evolution, when thieves make up the rules, and compassionate ones must break them, but must do so in quantum quantities without being noticed. Our prayer is that you take these times most seriously with tremendous humor; you see yourself as critical to making a difference globally and smile knowing you will. Do not accept that which you cannot change, but accept the fact that there's a way to change everything . . . smile, because you're the one who'll find the way.

$\mathcal{S}$ince the atomic revolution of the middle twentieth century, many children are being born with hyper-sensitivity. This is an evolutionary reaction to the reality that humans could annihilate themselves . . . a reaction of nature to the wholesale insanity of not seeing everyone as equal. You are most certainly amongst these hyper-sensitives, caught in the "stranger in a strange land" syndrome all your life. Yogi Bhajan would love to say, "Don't try to fit in, you fit perfectly in you." The signals of life's connections, equilibrium and balance, equality of all things, is obvious to your hyper-sensitivity when you allow it to flourish. But this is not normal in the present violently insecure civilization, with education, media, religion, and politics all constructed to support the military options. It's your responsibility to imagine a world without these violent options and to use your intuitional senses to find the doors into this imaginary world. Keep this imagination alive in the face of loss, and take action to recreate the alternatives that make the imaginary world real. Nikola Tesla once said: "If you want to find the secrets of the universe, think in terms of energy, frequency and vibration." This is the imaginary world . . . only termed imaginary because it's not three and four dimensional . . . can't be seen, heard, or touched, but it's actually there all the same. Quantum physics has demonstrated that all matter, at its sub-atomic core, is actually just energy. This includes both sentient life, inanimate objects and all of the stars in space. Matter is -- in fact -- not matter at all. This means -- as the hyper-sensitives, born of the threat of atomic annihilation -- you'll discover the solutions within atomic energy itself. "Humee hum Brahm hum" -- "What is to be already is." The solutions are there within the problems. Our prayer is that you keep the faith; maintain your hyper-sensitivity; develop it even further though the process is quite painful, and as a result you'll become one of those who discovers the polarity to the "evil" of ignorance . . . the military attitude that's pillaging Earth.

*B*igotry, phobias and discrimination are territorially driven miscalculations within the human imagination. This has been going on for thousands of years with survival conflicts and tribal disputes over unrecognized kinship and conflicting land rights. Whenever a society takes advantage, or promotes a collective bigotry, then evolution reverses its flow -- becomes devolution -- a root to the word 'devil'. In other words, finding advantage in the miscalculation of human imagination -- promoting bigotry, discrimination, non-kinship and phobia -- is devolution . . . "the work of the devil." This produces such vast differences in the distribution of resources that the specie devolves and ultimately collapses. Working against the very core of life, this creates false discrimination against every part of life . . . and whenever a specie believes its survival depends on this bigotry and hoarding, it will destroy itself. There's never peace in this state of consciousness. "Peace is the acceptance of conflict," Lao Tzu professed. Conflict is the presence of differences and the very nature of balance. The greater the differences, the easier the balancing act becomes. This is why a person, walking on a tight-rope, uses a long pole for balance . . . this pole (polarity) represents these differences . . . the longer the pole, the easier it is to balance. Acceptance of conflict is not doing nothing in the midst of it, it's using the conflicting polarities to neutralize their imbalances. This is the nature that bigotry and discrimination ignore. Acceptance of conflict -- fully comprehending the complete nature of the conflict and possesses the keys to its solutions. Acceptance inserts these keys into the lock -- opens the doors to a new vantage that then demonstrates where an advantage is. The obligation of evolution is to share this advantage with everyone . . . not hoard it. Our prayer is that you own the advantage of sharing; that you serve others in ways that promote this natural flow; that you develop a habit to know the devil when you see it, and then produce the polarity to its ignorance . . . one that's greater than its ignorance . . . for the devil is clearly present in these current times.

"I am, therefore I am," is a common teaching amongst the greatest masters of enlightened consciousness throughout human history. The root of these teachings of "I am" is found in nearly every language, in some form or another, and it means that the "I" is what "is" . . . the basis in the existence of the "self". That self which is experiencing this experience of existence is the 'I am'. In order to have such a clear experience, one must be free from the psycho-emotional distortions; to be free from anything that would interfere with such a sensitivity. Interpretations of any experience serve the intellect -- the actual experience of the experience serves the soul. This is the basis of the teachings of "I am" -- one who experiences the experience of the soul. Every language has a word -- or two -- for this "I am". In 'Aramaic', the language spoken two thousand years ago, the word for "I am" was Yahushua; it was Yeshua in Hebrew; iesous in Greek, and 'je suise' in Latin/French, all meaning "I am". This was, and is, a base teaching of great traditions . . . a mantra for meditations to be chanted, or thought of in silence. It's the basic message of an experience of the soul, the 'I am' -- the 'Yahushua' -- the 'Yeshua' -- the 'Yes'. It's this "Yes" -- that's the exclamation of experiencing existence . . . the soul in the body of existence . . . the yes I am . . . the Je Suise . . . the Yeshua . . . the Jesus. To have this profound experience, you must be completely clear in your consciousness . . . you must be clear like crystal. The word crystal comes from the root word krystallia in Greek -- which means ice. Krishna, in ancient Sanskrit, means crystal, or clear like ice. Such is the realization of the "I am clear" -- the 'Yahushua Krystallia' -- the 'Jesus Christ'. A statement of fact spoken from the soul . . . common to all life . . . an expression of pure existence in a physical body. Our prayer is that you experience this clarity today as the new light of the sun is born from its furthest point of the winter solstice; that you look into all these stories and see yourself in them all with the sacred eyes of inclusion, and give the gifts of the "sun's" love . . . the "yes I am crystal clear" with every breath you breathe.

The flower of life is a continuous intertwining of the seeds and flowers that are forever present in full presence . . . the essence and pressures that existence displays in the petals within the seeds. Like the truths in oral teachings -- the ancients used rhymes and rhythms to convey their mutable times with unmovable truths most effectively. But now in written teachings there's constant interpretation, and where symbols and signals are interpreted, they're always misunderstood. By default, human interpretations will rely on comfort to draw its conclusions. When symbols and signals have oral teachers they're not interpreted, and comfort never comes into the picture . . . truth is understood as an essence of pressure. This is why it's said, "The difference between mythology and history is that mythology is true." Even in the myths of dark and uncomfortable times, the characters were displayed in layers of symbology, and the destiny unfolded without the interpretations of pride. The "Once upon a time," was upon time, not within the time that was influenced by the times. Time is a layer without a reflection; the comfortable "self" is invisible in the darkness that prevails, but the castles with their solutions created angles in these layers of the land that wasn't land -- in a time that wasn't time. Directions wrap up in the depths of this perspective and the variables of what is to be . . . already are. It fits into the experience of whenever you are . . . that's the truths in the mythology sort of thing. At the moment of now, all of this has been lost for a very long time, and as these times go ever darker, the light of understanding is replaced by the darkness of interpretation . . . truth becomes that which you convince someone of and all that is gained is lost from the mirror . . . no clear reflections are visible in the darkness of misinterpretations. Our prayer is that you move back into the moment of now -- be present in your presence; learn from great teachings without interpretations; live in such truth without an opinion so that right is known by its light . . . transactions that have gain without loss, and the seeds of forever are giving birth the flowers of life.

When you find your way out of the current limitations of three dimensional space and the fourth dimension of time, you'll be free in the freedom of envelopment wrapping around the entire moment. Envelopment is the time and space of total equilibrium, balance, and union (yoga). Envelopment is an intuitive leveraging; it's a masterful observation that sees what truly is and not the distortions of what seems to be . . . distorted by personal agendas. It's the quality of absolute comprehension combined with a total sense of empathy and compassion. This is the new evolution, an evolution preparing for the future beyond this current catastrophe. It's not a new system, or a new organization -- it's an entirely new organism. The future is not about large organizations -- such as nations, religions, and corporations -- the future is about an independence gathered around deeply committed interdependence. It's about individuals with distributed connections and an enveloping embrace. It's about individuals operating in a field of distributed and completely compatible intelligence, not individually competing agendas, for the Earth is finding that the psychic weight of seven and a half billion personal agendas is far too much to bear. This is the nature of the new organism that's evolving, and this is why there's such a violent pushback, because it's removing your differences without making you all the same. But the fear is that you're losing something precious in the process. This is the natural fear that accompanies such great and global changes to the characteristics of the character. This is why there's violence around the world . . . the death throes of the old ways, and they're dying in a massive struggle to survive. This is the nature of evolution -- like water turning to steam when you've reached a sublimation point . . . a point of core-level transformation. Our prayer is that you're ready, willing, and able now to accept the change, challenge, opportunity and growth that's upon humanity; that you take a courageous role in this core-level event, and share love with the children to replace their natural fear with the faith that there's a way through . . . it will be OK.

Whenever the purpose of life is humane -- emotions are used as tools to gauge life, not guides that command and control it. When emotions control life, life goes out of control. There's a current pandemic of deep fearful ancient emotions -- more contagious than any physical disease – that's being abused by the powerful. This control will ultimately turn out of control in the unpredictable nature of the global wars -- where ancient emotions of sheer terror have been stirred into a suicidal peak . . . all in a time that fundamentally has nothing to fear. This current pandemic has been stirred up by the propagation of survival falsehoods . . . a tactic used by oligarchies throughout history to maintain control of the many, by the rule of the few. But this is the base nature of every failed evolution -- a few become 'superstrong' by false "measure" -- then extract all power from the weak, until the system collapses. It's the nature of every cancer -- the host, which in this case is humanity itself -- will ultimately perish. It's found in history . . . every system that's failed through bloated hierarchy -- every species that's fallen prey to consuming folly -- all unable to adapt to change. Dinosaurs became so large, they were annihilated by dramatic change . . . smaller and weaker creatures survived. When emotions and instincts evolve undisciplined, there's this danger that every species faces. Now is the time where humans face this identical fate. Look around the world and you can see the very few, the most powerful of all the humans by current measures -- which is money -- are gathering crowds around common goals of "surviving". Such is the nature of crowds, religions, nations, cultures and corporations. The challenge of demise is not in the core of these institutions, but in the emotional and instinctual immaturity of their memberships, and the disadvantage of the advantage taken by the leadership. Our prayer is that you educate yourself and others to become far more mature; to recognize that it's not survival of the fittest, but the strength of the many that creates prosperity, and when prosperity is distributed, the entire system prospers.

*T*he human brain is nearly ninety percent water . . . a biological fluid filled with neurology. It's flexible, extremely adaptive . . . an organ with highly coherent abilities. In order to maintain stability; accuracy of thinking and strategizing; memory storage and recall within this fluidity, there must be synchronization that's consistent. There's space between the surface of the Earth and the outer ionosphere known as the Earth-Ionosphere-Cavity (EIC). The ionosphere is electrically charged positive and the Earth's surface carries a negative charge, which produces an electrical tension that's discharged in thunderstorms. It sets in motion an extremely low frequency wave that's constantly circumnavigating the Earth. The wavelength of 7.83 Hz fits most easily into this (EIC) space, which becomes Earth's most dominant standing wave . . . known as the Earth's (Schumann) resonance, and an electro-magnetic field. This is also the exact resonance of the human brain in a deeply relaxed state . . . known as the 'theta-state' . . . the frequency of the human brain when dreaming and in deep meditation. Ancient masters have known for thousands of years, and now science is speculating -- this electro-magnetic field surrounding the Earth, can record thought waves and act as a global mind. It's a recording mechanism with the capacity to organize and influence collective human consciousness. This global mind has access to the universal mind . . . it's a relay system. When the brain is operating at this level of deep meditation, it accesses the global mind, which in turn accesses the universal mind. This indicates there's an incredible human capacity of enlightenment to influence the collective consciousness of humanity. The way you assist this is to meditate often and let your brain operate at this frequency as long as possible. Our prayer is that you're a participant in this human ability to influence the global human consciousness; that you're not absorbed by the frenetic, psychotic news babble, and your brain is free to access the universal mind with enlightening influence on the global mind and humanity. Become the change you want to see.

A river meanders across the lands -- does not always appear to be heading toward its destination, and yet a river is always already at the destination. Therefore, when not heading toward it . . . it's always heading to it. The balance sheet of all life contains assets and debts . . . this is the karmic record of lifetimes. No matter good, or bad -- life is always reaching for liberation . . . awareness of this is a compassionate life. When you're aware that a person -- no matter how badly they're behaving -- is making their way to their destination of liberation, you have more understanding of who they might be in any moment. The soul is the power that moves life; the spirit is that which retains life; the mind is that which explains life; the emotions are that which feel life, in a physical body that contains life. These are the elements involved with the "rivers of life" . . . the time it takes for each river to arrive at the ocean of liberation depends on the coordination of all these elements. Imagine then -- when you meet someone who's a complete jerk, a total mess, or worse . . . they're not just having a bad day, they could be having a bad lifetime. The spirit that retains you, also retains individual consciousness and its relationship to universal consciousness. This connection equals your accuracy. Normal attitudes desire more accuracy, and think of debts and mistakes as bad, but the nature of balance is in the balance. The Universe is balanced . . . everywhere, and in everything. Rather than considering someone's bad behavior and debts as bad -- consider it in reverse . . . as unpaid loans attempting to coordinate the investment of life. The Universe perceives debt as value . . . the power of assets over time that are equal to capacity. Otherwise, nothing but perfection could exist. This is the nature of compassion -- the pathway of an understanding consciousness. Our prayer is that when the rivers seem to be heading in an entirely wrong direction -- remember it's being guided through the topography of all life, by the universal gravity of all life, toward the ocean of all life . . . and it's already there . . . compassion remains aware of this truth.

*T*he music of the spheres are deeply harmonic vibrational streams -- created by what the great scriptures refer to as, "the Lord of the Cosmos." It is, in fact, created by waves in tubes of gravity, stretching between planets, stars and galaxies, producing harmonic intervals that conduct the laws of nature, and support the consistency of all matter. Like strings on gigantic instruments, it's been heard by sages, masters, prophets and great composers throughout time. Even Mozart, Bach, John Lennon and Paul McCartney, all claimed they never made up melodies . . . they heard them. Medical science knows that a musician's brain is wired differently, particularly a musician who's played as a child, long before the age of twenty-two when the brain stops rapidly developing. This brain seeks harmony in its world more than anything else. This is the nature of the music of the spheres -- master composers and spiritual prophets turned these ecstatic melodies into their compositions of music and poetic word-strings of scripture . . . ones that profess consistency, unity and agreement in life. This is why their music is loved and their teachings are followed. The great religious prophets were masterful in their enlightened lives . . . an awareness inclusive of everyone -- not judgmental of anyone; able to hear the harmonic intervals, and pathways that lead to this harmony in the midst of massive confusion and chaos. After passing from Earth, the area around where great Prophets lived still vibrates with this ecstasy. People flock to these locations; build shrines and make up rules for behavior. The great prophets were inclusive, but followers are often exclusive in the only way they can interpret an ecstasy they don't understand. Followers often can't hear the same music, or experience the harmony within "chaos", so they attempt to control the "chaos" with restrictive rules of behavior. Our prayer is that you listen consciously; set time aside to observe the harmonies of inclusive unity, and nurture pathways to their mastery . . . become a prophet of the new evolution and dance to the music of the spheres . . . it's playing your song.

Anyone who still believes that humans are a superior form of life on Earth is not paying attention. All life interrelates outside this 'human-defined' hierarchy of superiority . . . they relate in a 'mono-archy' of equality . . . all at the same level. If you look deeply into the eyes of any animal, you'll experience them viewing you as equal -- not their master. When you miss this, you miss the relationship . . . you miss the connection beyond the surface of your roles. Your task, in these times of great human insanity, is equilibrium. Your task in the experience of equilibrium, and the equality of all life, is to teach this by example to all that you can. Not to create a defiant opposition to the thoughts of human superiority, but to create the opportunity of an 'alternative' view in the minds of those who've been indoctrinated by the survival meme. Humans are biologically herbivores; everything about the human bio-system is that of a plant-eater. This was altered by several catastrophic events over the eons. Whenever the human ancestors ventured into the north, and the ice-ages descended upon them, all the plant-stock of good foods would disappear. In these life-threatening moments, for which there was no other answer, the humans and their ancestors took up killing and eating animals. With this ability to kill and the construction of weapons over time, came the idea of superiority . . . a false conclusion that has been the attitude of every victorious army throughout human history. Just because you can use weapons and kill others, does not make you superior. The human being will not survive with this attitude of superiority. It will only survive when it accepts itself as an equal amongst life and respects life. This will reduce the human activity that's polluting and destroying and begin to conduct life in harmony. Our prayer is that you lead this movement; that you act as an example of equilibrium amongst all life, and that you show the incredible health and value of the exquisite meals in a plant-based diet. Live as humans were created to live . . . stewards of this Earth, not as superiors who are devouring it.

*T*here are magnetic gauges in volcanic rock off the coast of Hawaii that indicate shifts in the Earth's polar fields occur at least every two hundred and fifty thousand years. The earth's north-south alignment today, is not where it was throughout history. The magnitude of such shifts could actually displace the tectonic plates, which would be catastrophic to all life on the Earth's surface. Discoveries over the past ten years indicate that an extinction-level cataclysm occurred between 12,800 and 11,600 years ago. This event was global, but its implications are not yet in the common conversations amongst published historians and archaeologists. All of these recent revelations seem likely to correlate with the myths, common around the world, of great human -- "golden ages" -- that were destroyed by massive floods and fire . . . that entire advanced civilizations within the 'human story' were eliminated, without trace, during such cataclysmic times . . . sending them back into the caves of protection. It's known that evolution relies on these crisis principles as a core reality -- they combine with the ingenuity of confrontation to stimulate and advance change. As the structure of universal intelligence, these moments respond to crisis by accessing hidden realities for solutions. All Earths -- throughout space -- and all of their abundant life, depend on these solutions to evolve beyond their perceived limits. Now is such a moment on this Earth -- only this time it's caused by human activity, which has very likely [also] occurred in the past -- and the only question is . . . are you on the side of the problem, or the solution? The solution must match the potential cataclysm . . . there are no comfort zones to hide in now, so if you're comfortable, you're definitely not paying attention. The messaging of this coming time is a game changer. Our prayer is that you take on the role of a solution; that you use your brain and your emotions to access the answers beyond your own life and begin living for all life. Now is the time to operate outside the linear thinking and emoting that got you here . . . become the awareness that will carry life out of here.

If you are not experiencing yourself as being everywhere, then where are you, and what do you experience when you're experiencing that you're not where you are? Where are you when you experience your experience and don't experience it everywhere? Such are the questions of existence that the Buddha posed to himself. Believing you're in some places and some moments, and not in others, he called the cruelty of duality . . . the illusion of limitation. This is the nature of being impossible . . . the nature of not experiencing all life as a relationship with all space and all time. Your task is to realize that right now is your opportunity to experience everything as possible; that your intention is a handle onto which this quest of life can grasp, and the results of your grasp will either follow this intention, or the chatter of limitation held in your brain. Do this: pose an intentional quest into this chatter and breathe . . . not like you're taking the breath, or even owning it, but as if you're receiving a gift. Receive this gift of breath at the very tip of your nose, and sit in the middle of the resulting sensation as the focus of this gift. Become the experience of breathing, not the breather, or the producer, and when you've experienced this meditation for a few minutes, you'll begin to experience yourself as the center of your existence . . . and then like you're everywhere. Eventually your psyche can gain access to the 'collective universal mind' and then you experience yourself everywhere. This becomes the foundation of intuition. The 'collective universal mind' is like an ocean -- there to serve you with every piece of knowledge you require. This form of conscious breathing is like the pass-code to this infinite database. Learning to use this properly is how intuition can guide you through the brain chatter and other chaotic forces that are always around in life. Our prayer is that you practice and learn to use your breath to power your intentions through the constant chatter of this world; that you add this meditation to your daily practice, and in this gentle silent way, discover yourself everywhere.

When driving in a car, you have no real sense of the tension, pressure, stress, and friction required on the car to make the drive. You're separated from, "where the rubber meets the road", and if you weren't, you may never drive. Yet this shock is what you experience when real awareness of life has no distractions to absorb the shock. There's a need to separate awareness and empathy from the punishment of the awareness . . . a way to consciously understand exactly what's taking place without suffering the impact of the emotional dynamics. In today's world however, there's so much separation from the realities of the "road" that empathy has been removed from the experience entirely. Humanity allows twenty-seven thousand children to starve around the world each day, while tons of food are discarded from stores because of blemishes in their appearance. It's clearly time to get in touch with some of the tensions, pressures, stresses, and frictions involved in the drive through life, without giving up the joys. This requires balance in your living experience; to be empathic toward all that's taking place on Earth, while still enjoying the experience of living on Earth. This is the purpose of the intuition beyond your emotions and feelings; this is the art and science of being empathic, without being devastated by your awareness. Balance and equilibrium are the keys; mastering the art of being human, while experiencing the science of being humane. This is the task required right here and right now, as one person's profit threatens another person's water rights; as one person's belief systems feel threatening to another person's sense of safety, and as seven and a half billion people try to live on Earth -- some of the shock needs to be experienced by all. There's a way to absorb the shock of the drive in life from the purpose of the drive . . . shield life without ignoring life. Our prayer is that you feel the shock of the human impact on Earth; that you gain traction from this experience, and make the determination to become empathic and aware, while maintaining your joy. This comes with a daily practice of higher consciousness and calmer communication.

The great unifier between emotions, and the vast intelligence and your interactive intellect, is the voice right there in your throat. When you open your throat with the sound of your voice, you can create harmony, or discord in your world inside and outside. It's not only the words you speak, but also the tones, rhythms and melodies with which you speak them . . . all of this is captured in the art and science of your voice. Humans are the only animal on Earth who create consonants . . . all creatures create vowels. Vowels produce the sounds and consonants cause the direction through which the sound travels. The human vocal anatomy is the most complex, with seventeen separate muscle groups in the tongue alone . . . the strongest muscle in your body. The fascia of the tongue connects directly to the muscles of the heart -- the voice connects your brain, the tongue and throat, and the neurology in the heart. This is why you speak and kiss with the tongue . . . all activities that produce connections. This is also why your dogs and cats lick you. Can you imagine all that comes through your tongue into the world? As you begin blending your emotions and intelligence you impact your environment. This is the purpose of mantras . . . combinations of syllables that impact the inner environment in a clear, actual and physical way. All words, including mantras are made up of the consonants and vowels. It's always said, it doesn't matter so much what a mantra means as what it does. The exact combination of vowels and consonants within each mantric syllable uniquely harmonizes intelligence, intellect, and emotions. This relaxes the physical body into greater ease; opens the intuition so the kundalini can rise through this ease with joy and knowing into a clearer understanding of solution. Our prayer is that you realize the power you have in your voice; that you use this power and the sound of your voice to influence the world around and the world inside; that you spend time each day speaking, singing and chanting with joy, and use this unique human capacity to become uniquely humane. In dark times, don't add to the darkness . . . be the light . . . be the voice.

*H*umans on Earth use sympathy . . . no other creature has this emotional tendency as strongly as humans do. Sympathy is an evolutionary feature, when used in proper dosage, it leads to experiencing empathy, which can then become compassion . . . all strong attributes. This evolutionary structure in addition to being an advantage, can also become a trap -- needing and feeding sympathy can create false emotional 'fulfillment-looping'. In the presence of exhaustion, discouragement, disappointment, betrayal and other similarly charged sensations, sympathy can fulfill an emotional need and diminish one's extra effort. Without strong monitoring, these false measures can dominate in very sophisticated ways . . . not the least of which is a propensity to almost succeed. Nearly succeeding brings great swells of sympathy, and when the comforting experience of sympathy exceeds the more arduous and painful efforts of success, there's an inherent conflict. Since sympathy can entrain empathy, and empathy can ultimately turn into compassion, there's also great purpose when used properly and managed, but if left without conscious management this instinct to avoid pain becomes defeating. One of the signs of this unmanaged syndrome is found in repeating patterns. When failures occur in similar ways over time, it's time to dig into these patterns. Discover the common threads in the patterns. The psyche and emotional body will attempt to hide these threads by blaming failures on circumstances, timing, and other people, but the common denominator is always clear evidence . . . these are personal patterns. Humans must maintain a balance on this sympathy asset; it's essential for everyone wanting to consciously grow. Our prayer is that you monitor all moments of exhaustion, betrayal, discouragement, and disappointment to make certain they're valid; whenever you hold anyone, or anything else responsible, triple check this claim against your emotional needs. Realize there's actually a more advanced path to empathy and compassion and swear off the use of sympathy . . . for like a candy bar, sympathy is a quick fix, but it's not an actual meal.

Quantum science recognizes the reality of time is a single moment . . . past, present, and future are one, a continuum where nothing's ever impossible. This has zero limits unlike the fourth dimension of perceived time and yet there's a relationship. It's this relationship that determines your sense of progress; determines your relation to hope . . . a sensation beyond space and time. Hope determines your mood; mood determines perception, and perception determines your sense of perceived time. This circular time-pattern is controlling -- just below the surface -- most human actions and interactions. This is why the zero card, the key of the Tarot deck -- a system of divination -- is the Fool. The 'Fool' is capable of opening these locks of perception to realms of real-time's continuum while living in the 'fantasy-prison' of three and four dimensions. Within these limited dimensions there are strict governing laws; one of these is 'Newton's Third Law of Motion' . . . "for every action, there's an equal and opposite reaction." . . . there's always a polarity of forces. This holds people back from actualizing their most outstanding abilities. The Fool, according to mythologies, never knows when their being insulted, and therefore cannot be hindered by any negative reaction to their actions. This is a position you must take if you're going to live an outstanding life . . . of standing out from the crowd. For whenever you're outstanding, there'll be equal forces pulling you back inside the parameters of being "normal" -- of being "smaller" -- of being more practical and "realistic". This is the time to be un-cautious, but not unconscious . . . this is the path of the Fool . . . small focused steps producing outstanding moments without stumbling. Our prayer is that you're the perfect 'Fool' in your outstandingness; that you throw yourself into time and life, in order to have the most upstanding time of your life; that you escape the 'fantasy-prison' of limiting dimensions and foolishly deflect the reactions to your greatness.

There's an old saying, "A little knowledge is a dangerous thing." A little knowledge believes in perfected dances with performance patterns based on the limited views of seemingly seamless habits. This unique sense of self is supported with language and phrasing that intellectually supports this "security". But within such a brain-dominated environment, actual change and growth is difficult -- deep changes to the where, why and how you're existing feel threatening, and are defended against with fancy word strings of perceived "great" knowledge. Herein lies a dilemma for real growth, which is often the aimless motion through gaps in time into unknown spaces of chaos. When perception is focused on "knowingness", and language supports this little knowledge . . . the required gaps don't appear, and false knowing defends the seamlessness. The inherent problem in such a "perfected" dance is like the problems of breeding a single bloodline -- weaknesses are multiplied and go unnoticed -- there's no polarity, or opposition to define them. Polarity and strong opposition creates an inner strength that confidently permits change and needed growth. Enter a deeply committed relationship, one that disrupts this false knowledge with appropriate mirroring, and does so with authority . . . this is the power of committed love; the power of a relationship in which there's no open exits; this is the power of being cornered by the promise of forever. All the information required for change is present in every moment, but true change takes place when equilibrium is challenged -- this is the deeper nature of evolution. True growth can be chaotic, random, confusing and presented with anxiety. None of these options are attractive to a perfection dancer, but all of these options are present in a "cornered" relationship . . . a fully committed partnership. Our prayer is that you welcome the disruption of love to receive love; that you relax your dance just enough to allow the missteps of partnering to gain a foothold, and that you welcome the unknown into your knowledge base . . . awakening is endless . . . commit to forever.

*B*eing ready is an opportunity that's common in every moment to act upon, not an opportunity to wait for. There's an ancient proverb, "Ready is the belief within a moment, not a moment somewhere in time." Being ready is the courage -- the position of your heart -- that's commonly available to everyone . . . an act of facing all the fears, concerns, doubts and hesitations until they're no longer in control. A master once said that ready is facing the flames of life until they bow down to your life. Ready is connecting with your greatest projection . . . not being limited by your need for protection. The present moment, in the construction of time, is the movement of space through your perspective. The moments of the past are always right there, they've passed through, and the moments of the future are always right there . . . right before you. "What is to be, already is" (Humee Hum Brahm Hum) . . . when you're not ready now, you're not ever ready. Until you make readiness active, your readiness is simply sleeping. This is not to imply that fears, concerns, doubts and hesitations have no value -- they're what makes the final version so much better than the first draft; they're what keeps you painting until the art is creatively complete; they're what improves your skillsets toward their ultimate performance. The way you work with these emotions will either guide your life, or block it . . . they either make up your weakest parts, or they work with weakness to become strength. All in the angle of perception, the idea of ready and the idea of time are parallel. Like the common 'South Asian' phrase, "Just now coming," commitment is the antidote that overrides these perception codes from deep history. It allows you to present to this present moment that being unready is actually being nearly ready. Our prayer is that your readiness is just now coming and in fact nearly ready; that your fears, concerns, doubts and hesitations are sharpening your skills, not denying that you have them; that your commitment knows you're ready in the complete picture of time, and that it's working at all times to complete this picture.

Depression is not deep sadness, it's the Universal consistencies of tension, pressure, stress, and friction in search of the Universal efficiencies of ease, joy, knowing, and liberation. An inspired life is not a direct assault on depression, it's a natural result of these Universal natures . . . a play between consistencies and efficiencies. In weather, this same play creates the winds -- a differentiation in pressures -- one of which is called a depression. In life, the "winds of change" are also caused by these differentiations and one of them is also called depression, but it's not a bad thing . . . it's just a thing. 'Wahe Guru' is an ancient expression meaning GOD that uses this same differentiation within its structure. 'Wahe' simply means wow, but 'Gu' means darkness . . . 'Ru' means light. 'Guru' is the total light that comes from total darkness . . . everything comes from absolute nothing. Wahe Guru exclaims, in this fantasmalogical creation of the Cosmos where there's far more space inside yourself at any moment than there is outside yourself in every moment . . . you're actually made of light inside nothing. Realizing your body is light is one way to lift natural depression . . . your body, and everything about the physical Earth, is the dust of light from the sun. When you slow down your rhythms, you begin to touch these Universal efficiencies that take advantage of this light that's you. These Universal efficiencies are not about speed, they're about connection, traction, grip and accuracy, yet they fulfill their time-lines as fast as light. There's a Native American fable: a young child asks the Grandmother how long it will take to accomplish a task. "Well," she answers slowly, "It should take about a week if you set your mind to it, but if you really hurry, it will take two weeks." Our prayer is that you take the time it takes to connect; that you allow these connections to bring about the winds of change; that you don't dwell in the pressures of depression, but ride their winds into inspiration and allow the ease, joy, knowing and liberation, that's always inspired, to be always here . . . right here . . . right now.

Life's a reflection -- "holes" and "potholes" are an indispensable part of this 'whole' picture reflection. But whenever you find yourself inside familiar and repeating holes you must stop and question. Ask yourself to examine the deeper patterns behind this repeating history. These patterns are facets in your interpretation of time, the facets you'll rarely look directly at -- even avoid -- until you can't. Then, when you're no longer able to ignore their patterns, it's usually when you're back inside another hole that feels just as familiar and your energy is being consumed with survival . . . which feels immensely purposeful and meaningful . . . once again, however, the cause disappears amongst the symptoms. Are you dedicated to the sense of extreme purpose that comes from surviving these "black" holes? Are you addicted to the blame that's a constant reaction to these "life-threatening" forms of lessons? Are you searching the horizons for the reasons rather than acknowledging the common denominator in the repetition? These are healthy questions to question. Sometimes life attempts to decorate your holes; make them look seasonally different, unique from moment to moment, or even livable, but it's far better to realize that these holes are clues to your deeper character patterns. These repeating patterns are the methods evolution uses to explain your life to your life. They're maps of your deepest weaknesses so they can be healed, and life can resolve all the great depression patterns around these holes with definitive warnings . . . you'll see the holes coming before you fall in. Our prayer is that you take full and total responsibility for the holes you fall into; when you're in a hole, explore the entirety of the hole to remove any patterns that attach you to these repeating loops; that you own the holes, discover the familiarities and similarities in your history, and then chart a path with discipline markers to not repeat the patterns. Once you climb out, use these same climbing skills to master the mountains . . . the goals that are everywhere in your life are right there, right now.

There's a cosmic chatter around everything; a collective-etheric conversation that denotes and promotes the purpose and vision of it all . . . all the reasons of every detail directly corresponding to the intention of each existence. When you're in touch with this chatter; when you're aligned with this conversation around you, there's very little resistance in your life . . . most everything unfolds with ease. This holds true throughout the layers of time, and whenever resistance to progress appears, you must remember, resistance is only resistance when it's resisted. When it's embraced, it transforms into a form of this cosmic guidance. Guided by this cosmic chatter, life can carry your intentions in directions outside your intention; counter to your pre-determination, and resistance creates chaos. It's at these moments you must use the energy of this guidance, and re-establish your direction, for these forces are to be used, not to be confused or disrupted by . . . resistance is only resistance when it's resisted. Only an angle of interpretation stands between what appears as chaos, and a conclusion that realizes your intention. It's up to you to trust the guidance of the chatter; it's up to you to allow the energy of all resistance to become a partner in transformation, for even though you're not certain of the new formation, count on its alignment to your overall intention and use it. After all, the Cosmos knows who you are, where you are, and what you want to be. This is the law of nature -- a cosmic principle, and you are not outside nor being forgotten by this . . . not an exception to this rule. Resistance is a part of the guidance that surrounds your intentions . . . use the guidance. Our prayer is that when confronted by resistance, you look more deeply into its nature and discover the guidance it's offering; that when you're confronted by the opposition, you see it as energy for transformation and use it; that you appreciate this cosmic chatter that surrounds everything as just part of purpose . . . tune into it and build momentum with it. Let the resistance of opposition be an insistence of your purpose . . . this is the chaos of nature.

Changing the world is a task that some have accomplished in parts. Cecil Rhodes and Steve Jobs are contrasting examples of world change. Cecil Rhodes created the Rhodes Scholarships -- using the DeBeers diamond fortune and Oxford University -- to exclusively influence the hierarchies of governance. Steve Jobs created hand-held devices that disassemble hierarchies with an inclusive free-global exchange of information. The formula is exacting, not "loosey-goosey" -- global change requires profound technologies (internal and/or external), and attitudes that sustain this technology for a lasting impact. The religious prophets are an example of internal technologies . . . their effectiveness was in how they lived their lives. For real and lasting change, a "portion" of the world must be aware of it; a portion of that portion must realize it; a portion of that portion must fully actualize it, and a portion of that portion must master this actualization and teach it to others. The idea of these portions was first described in the Bhavishya Purana by Vedic wisdom keepers living thousands of years ago. Their formulas were committed to writing in Sanskrit and speak in percentages of the global population. The underconscious are unable to comprehend, or even consider a higher consciousness. The semiconscious freely speak of it, but are unwilling to actually experience it . . . unwilling to relinquish their personal priorities. The conscious are willing to connect with their higher consciousness, and then there's a smaller percentage willing to fully discipline, master and teach it. In the past, these masters were quickly iconized and worshipped instead of being mimicked and duplicated. The common path of every major religion runs through this worship of a Master . . . not mimicking and duplicating the mastery. The fact that you're reading this means you're capable of duplicating a mastery. Our prayer is that you apply yourself to your discipline; work toward achieving a mastery that suits you; create a daily practice and practice it daily . . . the world is waiting to change from the example of your highly conscious changes.

*T*here's a power in the darkness of these darker times that's forcing courage into daily practice. 'Cour' means heart, and 'age' means time . . . courage approaches the world from the heart. The heart has neurology imbedded in its muscles -- considered another brain, it's to be more fully developed in the new evolution. The heart-brain is not exacting and two dimensional like the head-brain; it explores tangents of tangents that can lead to outcomes with little to do with the original intent, then morph the original intent to follow the new opportunities that emerge. This courage of new dimensions looks beyond the two dimensions of right and wrong; good and bad; yes and no; reward and punishment. Being rewarded for doing right, at the expense of being adventurous, can destroy the path of discovery and eliminate potential solutions. Schools and cultures of the future will teach that faith and trust are found in this heart-brain, and to include these tangents rather than being critical and pushing them away. With this, the future can observe a connectedness beyond the impossibilities of two dimensions, ones that are insights and intuitions when viewed from the heart's higher-dimensional perspective . . . ones never explored in a culture determined by immediate results. This is the positive power of the heart's exploration through these dark times . . . an arduous, yet essential voyage into the tangents of tangents -- which morph intentions to match unusual outcomes -- which allow these outcomes to be steps toward original intentions with greater solutions far beyond the "narrows" of the two-dimensional thinking. This adventure shape-shifts characters through characteristics, and allows impossible relationships to transform into heartfelt ones. Though this makes no sense to your logical brain, it's far superior to logic . . . it's magic. Our prayer is that you discover this relationship in your magical heart; that you allow it to flourish without reward beyond your logical views, for this is the next evolution of human consciousness . . . the greater rewards of a magical life . . . the light in the darkness of these dark times.

*H*umans have developed their collective opinions around primitive emotions. It's an emotional body -- stuffed full of survival reactions -- that hasn't been advanced, upgraded, or revitalized for millions of years. Still operating in a perceived danger zone of three dimensions, these emotions hold little truth; are only opinions, but are wrapped in layers of ancient symbology that have zero relationship in modern language. They influence cultures through their symbolic default and dominate the collective subconscious without words. These opinions also desire survival and the collective emotional body supports this. Remember, the Earth was always round, but a "flat-Earth" lived in the fears of collective opinion for centuries. Today's darkness of bigotry, territorial insecurity, branding dissimilarities with xenophobia, all have these same deep roots of collective "reality" without facts. It's another 'post-truth, flat-Earth' era of primitive, unrealistic emotions. Even "cosmic" opinions imbedded in religions, cultures, and nationalism need liberating from their primitive emotional support . . . from the mythologies that fan the flames of intolerance. Astronomy is based on the visible three dimensions, but future dimensions -- not yet perceived by human senses -- will liberate many of these fixations about the Universe. The prophets of today's religions; other masters throughout history, and humans awakening at this very moment, all realize the only way to survival is cooperation throughout the collective body of life, not the exclusivity of emotional needs. The stories and critical opinions that support ancient survival emotions must be rewritten; scientific knowledge of this universe must be expanded . . . it's time to upgrade the human 'operating-system' and realize how endless 'infinity' actually is; just how necessary loving all life with humility actually is. Our prayer is for this systemic reboot; for a global realization that all life is interdependent with all life, and that this interdependence is the power of life's survival on Earth. "Tag" you're it . . . now be it, and do it.

Your physical life is coordinated by consciousness -- or spirit body, plus the focus of your brain -- the five regions of the mental body, and your feelings -- the emotional body. To manifest willfully, you must coordinate this human instrumentation. Most humans are just smart animals; very few can articulate or calibrate this power and miracle of being human . . . a power no other creature possesses. When the passion, from the emotional body, is focused through this matrix, there's nothing humanly impossible. But passion is normally unconscious, an unfocused emotion without controls . . . not a tool, but a weapon. Consciousness has two modalities: one is to create horizons, or expansions; the other is to produce a focal point . . . one pointedness. Horizons open exploration and the vast intuition. Focal points draw this in to understand and establish the next steps in any given moment. The direction of the eyes during meditation will establish which of these you use: mediations at the third eye point create horizons; meditations on the tip of your nose create a focal point. The five regions of the mental body are the subconscious, super-conscious and the conscious mind . . . with the conscious-mind subdivided into negative (inspective); positive (projective), and neutral (introspective). Meditations coordinate this . . . a master planner of life's game. Without a regular practice of meditation, life is just a ball in the game . . . rolling wherever it's kicked. Meditation on a daily basis makes you a player, a coach, and even an owner of the time of your life . . . able to draw the map of your life. The world around you is always going to be the world around you; like the weather, you have no control over this. How it affects you, and what you make of it -- this can be up to you. Our prayer is that, in the dark nasty storms of this time in the history of life, you build a habit of meditation to become a player, a coach, and the owner of your time; that you make choices from moment to moment about the depth, direction and purpose of your life, and that you give yourself the powers of your human ability each moment in your life . . . make nothing impossible.

In the times of Jesus and other great prophets, it was very much like today . . . empire building, disregard for nature, a massive concentration of wealth, and cruelty out of control. To be safe in such times of disregard for higher order, invasive pressures, and ultra-surveillance -- the disciples and Jesus, and every other great prophet in their own particular time of history, took to teaching, speaking and writing in allegory and code. Today these codes -- contained in all the stories that have survived -- are interpreted by misinterpretation and presented by misrepresentation as fragments of fact, and figments of fiction. This misses the deep lessons; disrupts the true meanings, and doesn't teach from the universal mind, but is wielded as a weapon of control. This is the current state of many religions around the world -- all based on the true enlightenment of a miraculous prophet, but now corrupted with confusion; misrepresented with competition while vying for a position in an arena that requires no positions. Consciousness is all you own, everything else is a rental . . . even your body is returned when life is over. Your consciousness can grow when these lessons are real, but when there's no concept of the true history of time, you have no relationship with the consequence of actions in the sequence of time. As life becomes disrupted by this misrepresentation of the prophets, this physical world becomes a dangerous place. False realities pervade throughout the underconscious hordes as the bullies take advantage, and there's always more underconscious than above it . . . always more students than teachers in a classroom . . . Earth is a one-room schoolhouse. Our prayer is that you stop questioning this reality and start addressing it; that you learn magical techniques for teaching with problem students and apply them in this world; that you take the opportunity of this current crisis and evolve your response to the point of miraculous, unexplainable . . . even unimaginable solutions. Be the wisdom-keepers; the light-workers, and the difference-makers this Earth requires, for now is the time, you are a prophet and you have no choice.

Seekers of awakening; students of infinity; practitioners of life's arts and sciences of consciousness often complain that meditation is not greeted by the pleasantness of openness; the attitudes of readiness, or a heartfelt sense of willingness, but instead are confronted by noise and blockages. This is because meditation disassembles old fixed patterns and reassembles them into ones that better serve new moments on the path of awakening. This is not always a dance -- sometime it's a struggle -- especially when you approach patterns that've become attachments. Like ploughing old land to plant new seeds, there are times when the plough strikes large rocks. These rocks are deeply attached to the ground right where they are; there are ancient reasons for each of these rocks -- attachments have deep meaning and their patterns hold the maps of many pathways you can put to great use. Most people's deep patterns have been in place, not just in this lifetime, but for incarnations. They're entrenched in the biology of generations; the cosmology of incarnations, not just the fantasy of this moment. The subconscious believes these attachments are protecting life itself, and will hold on for dear life. This is not the time to be concerned, but a moment to concentrate and discover the circles inside the attachments, and the cycles inside the desires . . . this is the discovery that will set you free. This is the entrainment of meditation -- not about getting it right, but getting right to it; not about proving who you are, but improving who you are. It's about being cognoscente of the rhythms, cycles, and circles of attachment and desire in relation to your experiences . . . allowing experience to touch meaning . . . to find purpose. Our prayer in these times of darkness: have a daily practice of meditation, and when it runs into rocks -- sit with the rocks to learn from them; when it runs into noise -- sit with the noise until it turns into the music of the winds and the spheres. Run with these winds; discover their magical harmonies . . . the rocks will show back up, again asking to be dissolved and resolved . . . after all, it's a meditation.

Consciousness relates space with time, and it's the key to liberating any restrictions of space and time. Consciousness holds the atoms, molecules and cells in the forms of their form, and yet -- when expanded further -- it accesses dimensions beyond these forms . . . the dimensions with all the solutions for these forms. Three and a half million years ago, human ancestors mastered standing up . . . after four million years of trying. Standing up introduced the third dimension of spatial depth, and with it came spatial movement and its interpretation as time. These two new dimensions solved many physical problems, even scarcity of food was solved as this expansion allowed for migration over greater distances where there was more abundant food. There's a new expansion in human consciousness; this time into dimensions only currently known in dreams . . . this is the new standing up . . . the new evolution. Your physical form is maintained, and this physical world is navigated by using the most basic levels of your awareness . . . your consciousness. It's been this way for millions of years, since the earlier developments of conscious reflection, when physical standing up fully introduced this third dimension of space and the fourth dimension of time. As the human brain delved deeper into measuring space and time, it developed 'economics' as a trusted system for tracking and measuring the movements. Trust is now breaking down . . . these economics don't serve all of life. With the introductions of new dimensions, there will also be a new economics . . . a new discipline for measuring and maintaining value. This is the current battle -- old traditions fighting new evolution . . . crisis will be the determining factor . . . trust will be the judge. This new standing up will again solve problems of life, and like the old standing up, those who doubt it, will fight it. With old traditional thinking, you won't recognize the new dimensions . . . you can't understand what you don't experience. Our prayer is that you become a pioneer of the new dimensions; travel and map them every day; learn from your mistakes and master your strengths, and become the trust that evolves.

"*L*ife does not happen to you, it happens through you." The light of perception from infinity, passes through you -- then reflects off your surrounding events and moments back to you. This is what you experience of the time and space that surrounds you. The events and moments you resist, or reject, will define you -- by the mere friction of this resistance -- more profoundly than that which you fully accept. To fully accept does not mean to fully agree with, but it means that you've not set up this resistance . . . you're allowing space and time to pass through you with acceptance. Then, within this acceptance, you have the power to make choices whether to agree -- be affected -- both -- or neither. These are the choices of freedom . . . choices important to the quality and consciousness of your life. Additionally -- by this same physical fact in the nature of light and perception -- nothing happens incorrectly, or by some other source of initiation. "If it happens to you, it happens through you," literally means that nothing appears without your directive. Obviously this directive can be conscious, or unconscious, and when it's unconscious there's disconnect and powerlessness. But once a conscious connection is established between your psycho-emotional awareness, and the world all around you, and you stop resisting the events with the moments, then life no longer appears as a stranger . . . no longer appears as the enemy . . . no longer appears to be happening to you . . . it is you. The events and moments passing through you that you embrace are what defines you, or not, by the power and freedom of this choice. This is the meaning of responsibility . . . the ability to respond. With this responsibility you're able to make good choices; the more you practice, the better you are at making these choices; the better you are at making these choices, the more life unfolds according to your wants and needs. Our prayer is that you take on this responsibility of being the leader of your life; that you welcome the freedom of choosing the qualities in each moment, and with this freedom of acceptance, you make decisions regarding your agreements. This is personal power.

*N*o matter what emotions are current, they originated, not in this moment, but possibly in moments not of this life -- not of this persona -- not even this situation. When your awareness does not encompass this entire picture, you'll attribute current feelings onto whatever's available . . . blame it on the "lowest hanging fruit", it's often said. All emotions come from a combination of inputs, some are sensory; some are memory; some are associative, or dissociative, and some are just made up from this "low-hanging fruit". Wild creatures smell through the winds of the moment; hear through the sounds within the sounds in the moment, and their responses are governed by instincts programmed to translate these signals without disruption from any accompanying "noise". They've evolved through this process of selection to have mastered these skills in their most accurate form. Humans, on the other hand, aren't limited to just instincts, but rely on memories; associative stories; countless sources that mix the senses of a moment, with the stored senses from other moments; then mix these translations with input from others . . . all managed by the attention, or exhaustion; inspiration, or desperation, and focus, or confusion that's present with the experience. It's like having a map-maker, who's also a great story-teller, and the roles are constantly mixed and matched to an audience. All measures in the maps become reactions to the stories -- accuracy not at issue, but entertainment is at the core. This is the human dilemma of feelings . . . stories of the past and present fail to be maps leading anywhere . . . they're reactions to actions that may, or may not have occurred, may be of memory, or anticipation, or even manipulation . . .

not a map to anywhere . . . just the whims of a clever "thief". These are today's unnatural times and nature is about to make corrections . . . climate change is "crowd" control. Our prayer is that as you recognize the winds of "insanity" with the accuracy at your core; that you experience the insane, then respond and interact from the sanity of this accuracy . . . be a guide for being found, in a world that's being lost.

If big capital is a problem -- it's also a solution; when corporations are a problem -- they're also the solution . . . everything has the polarity of itself, existing directly beside itself. This isn't currently practiced, but you're entering a new era of revelation and solution . . . a time of re-evolution that peeks through cracks in the fabric of time. Solutions to problems are found in these cracks that have been invisible. The best time to touch this alternate reality are the hours just before the rise of the sun. This darkness before the dawn is a time of infrared sunlight. This 'long-wave' light stimulates the 'theta-waves' -- the 'dreamtime' and 'deep-meditation' waves of the human brain. They coordinate with each other in imaginative ways, but once daylight arrives, it illuminates three dimensional matter and eliminates imagination. The brain further distorts these so-called "real" images with the fourth dimensional thoughts and feelings of time. The 'dreamtime' and 'deep-meditation' time are not limited to this so-called "reality" . . . they imagine beyond it where the solutions live. The evening used to also reflect this greater dimensional realm. It was rich with dancing shadows of fire and candlelight, and did this for hundreds of thousands of years since fire was first used . . . one-and-three-quarter million years ago. The human psyche molded these shadows into an imagination of evolution. The present world of incandescent lighting has changed these angles and screens of viewing. Elimination of the dancing shadows on the outside, has placed fixed shadows inside the mind . . . blaming others is the emotional reaction. In the softness of firelight there is no blame, just a deeper search for meaning in the images. Blaming is shallow -- it eliminates this imagery, and the solutions it holds. Our prayer is that you spend more time in the soft candlelight of evening's imagination; that you spend more time in the pre-dawn infrared time of intuition; that you discover the solutions which have never been imagined, and promote loving kindness throughout the sunlight each day.

"Tithai tuu samarath" -- the treacherous and impassible world is navigated generously with the sound and grace of the 'shabd' . . . the sacred mantras of wisdom. There are moments when you're climbing a mountain -- you look down at the trail and see so many different places to put your feet with each step you take. Each one of these steps will take you through a different set of circumstances, but they'll all eventually arrive at the top, or bottom, of the mountain depending on which way you going. The destination is common, but the adventures of the trail are unique. There are many unique adventures caused by the choices in each moment, but destiny is the ultimate outcome and this is guaranteed. Life is just such a mountain trail . . . sometimes you're ascending into your goals, and other times you're walking down for a rest. Each moment has choices -- different ways to view the experience and various places to step. With each choice you receive thoughts, feelings and emotions that dictate the sensations that you're experiencing, but this is not your experience, this is the illusion of observation. In the midst of this illusion, each moment can be considered a triumph, or a tumble – ease, or struggle – joy, or sorrow . . . this is the background of the illusion in time. Such is the path in the moments of time . . . a trail on the mountain of your life. The outcome is your destiny -- this is guaranteed, but the path through the moments is caused by the choices you make. No one is responsible for your experience in the illusion; no one controls the sequence of your events, and the sooner you have this realization, the faster you'll arrive at your destination. I once walked a mountain every morning with an elder 'wisdom-keeper' who was four times my age. He beat me up and down this mountain every day because . . . he said, "When I walk the mountain, I only walk the mountain." Our prayer is that while walking the mountain of your life, this is all you're doing; that you take full responsibility for the experience you're having, and make the most of wherever you are, whenever you're there. "Tithai tuu samarath" . . . sing for joy and you'll find it . . . it's a universal law.

There are two and a half hours before the rise of the sun, where the rays of arriving light are infrared. This is known to the yogis and masters as "amrit vela" the "ambrosial hours". This is the time when early light -- it's an invisible light -- carries vast quantities of information for nourishing life. Remote controls use this light to carry information. These are the longest rays in the light spectrum -- so long that they actually wrap around one-tenth of the Earth's curvature -- hence the two and a half hours before sunrise, which is one-tenth of a twenty-four hour day. Within these volumes of information this light carries, are the inclinations of the coming time that's interconnected to the time of this moment. When you're aware of these inclinations of the times to come, this ignites intuition from the time that is. These infrared rays are attuned to the longer "theta" waves of your dreamtime brain, which is the same state of the brain in deep meditation. Therefore these waves of sunlight, align with the waves of your meditation, which aligns with the information that's about to unfold in time . . . a perfect formation of intuitive clarity. What activities, or non-activities, are best for this time . . . ones that enhance the effects of this time? Stretching into your body-glove is one, as it increases the physical contacts of the nerves . . . nerves are awareness. Chanting mantras, which are syllables of sound, enables the brain to coordinate with these longer waves. Silent meditations allow the brain to observe the information without 'analysis chatter'. Deep conscious breathing produces direct access to these theta rhythms to focus without random noise. As a result, your body and mind are connected and aligned within time, not distracted by it. You tune into each moment that is, and then receive clarity for the times to come. Our prayer is that you are early into bed and early to rise . . . wise, like the saying goes; that this wisdom knows how to approach each moment with a successful plan, and that these plans benefit the world . . . create the changes that these times need to see. Rise up each day and become family.

*G*iving thanks is gratitude that connects with your highest level of openness, the level of receptivity that accepts your heartfelt desires. This goes beyond your needs, for all needs are met through a strong genetic predisposition to survive. Gratitude opens the dreams of destiny and desires to thrive; the fulfillments of life beyond the needs of life . . . recognized and received through the trust and gratitude of giving thanks. As has been known throughout physics -- for every action there's a reaction . . . equal and opposite. This happens in energy; happens in matter, and also in the actions around psycho-emotional choices. Along this line, there's an "odd" choice within the western Thanksgiving holiday (holy-day) . . . the "odd" traditional feast. As the saying goes -- so goes the biology, "You are what you eat." What are you when you eat turkey? The psycho-symbolic meaning of a turkey is, "to live with unrealized abilities." The ability of every bird is to fly; that's why they all have wings, but the turkey is a bird, with wings, but cannot fly. Eating turkey is therefore feeding all of your bodies the wrong food . . . you're enriching and nourishing your inabilities to fly. When you think of this in relation to gratitude and giving thanks, which enhances your abilities, these are working at cross purposes . . . they're mixed-fixed polarities. It's time to break the habits that disrupt your powers of gratitude and use this power of giving thanks to open the psycho-emotional systems to the dreams of your abilities, and the desires of your heart. Use the nature of these darkest times to fulfill those same laws of physics . . . enable the polarity of darkness. As the darkest hours are just before dawn, these are the hours that hold the most promise. The gratitude of giving thanks is a most certain path to opening the doors of dawn, and enabling your abilities of promise. Our prayer is that you give thanks for that which you've received, and for that which your heart still desires; that you allow this to shift your physical and psycho-emotional perceptions to receive that which your destiny deserves, and fulfill your dreams with thanksgiving.

The 'Five Treasures of the High Snow' is the fabled name of the third highest mountain in the world . . . Kangchenjunga. Every climber that's ever reached near its summit, has stopped just short to keep a promise to the Chogyal -- the monarchs of the former kingdom of Sikkim, from where this vast mountain rises. Kangchenjunga is actually five peaks, not just one, and the valley in the middle of these five peaks holds fantastic mythologies. Story says it's the entrance to a world of masters who live well over a hundred and fifty years . . . then incarnate where they're needed. According to the accounts of those who live at the base of this massive mountain, the lives of these masters are the nature of miracles. This mountain's base is so large, it borders India, Bhutan, Nepal and Tibet. The physical powers of such enormous masses of earth rising from the Earth is in the electromagnetic and gravitational fields they hold in their presence . . . so strong it affects infrared light. This is caused by a combination of magnetite in the molten magma, and the sheer gravitational size of the mountain itself. It's within this field of immense forces that the accounts of great mastery accompany mountains such as this. An example is the story of Rishi Dusht Daman, who incarnated three hundred years ago as Guru Gobind Singh. With the help of these massive mountain forces, these masters develop their ability to use infrared light in the superconscious mind to break up space and time into their subcomponent parts . . . revealing the three and four dimensions before their fully formed. This infrared spectrum is the silent intuition, without the slightest resistance, that also occurs in the two hours just before sunrise. This infrared intuitive superconsciousness can be accessed in the early morning on the waves of silence; on the waves of mantra; on the waves of yantra (visual mantras), and on the waves of deeply neutral contemplation. Our prayer is that you use the early morning hours as the mountain of your meditative life; that you view the future that's forming in the shadows of other dimensions, and then live your life in the grace of this knowing.

The depth of what's going on with masses of humanity is causing tremors throughout the psyche of the Earth. It's perhaps most visible in certain countries -- always in front of the news -- but this underconsciousness has been here since the beginning of time. The reason it's so vulnerable, delicate and dangerous now, even though it's always existed, is due to the electronics that are multiplying its effects. As is known, the vast majority of suicides are not an attempt to kill one's self, but an extreme call for help, the Earth at this moment is demonstrating this same extreme need. Every soul goes through this, you've been through it, and now there's a far larger crowd of humanity going through it. There's always two thirds of the total population in this underconscious condition. Just as throughout much of nature, there's more offspring than adult animals and plants, during the birthing season . . . to insure survival. Within the evolution of the soul, there are also birthing seasons, and during them there's larger numbers at the beginning than there are at the end of mastery. Right now is the birthing season, and two of three humans are newborn . . . they're underconscious beginners looking just like you, but they're more innocent than you. They're more delicate, vulnerable, and impressionable, and to hide this they use aggression and false arrogance . . . just like a child. An individual, or group of individuals can easily influence them into a mob with images of false danger and this is now happening. For every action there's reaction, but today's reaction to this underconscious wave has been weak because higher-consciousness is nonaggressiveness and far less emotionally charged. Our prayer is that you're aware you are superconscious; time to become super active without aggression, but with motivated intentions; that you activate your devotional body to neutralize the emotional bodies filling Earth's blogosphere; that you ignite your devotions of inspiration not excitement; enthusiasm not aggression; faith not fear, and love not hate, for the scales of justice and balance depend on you now more than ever.

There's an old saying, "The difference between mythology and history is that mythology is true." Myths are the stories of fact that've been told in symbols, they have no language of facts. The language of facts is a limited, often two dimensional language. Mythological stories are from dimensions beyond what "facts" can describe. Take a famous story in the Bible, the story of Adam and Eve. It's actually the story of the 'Atom' (matter in now) and the 'Eve'ntual' (matter of future-now). There's the part where Adam's rib creates Eve. The deeper myth is that the rib used was the seventh rib -- the rib that connects the heart center to the outer world. The heart center -- the center of reflective engagement -- is the center of relationship. This is where you manifest your partnership with the attributes you require to unfold your destiny . . . from your heart. Mythology presents a shorthand version of the symbology conversing between your brain and the universal mind . . . pictures worth a thousand words. The conscious 'brain-mind' connection has been programmed over thousands of years to work in the language of words, but it didn't always. Words are open to interpretation, and the interpretations are also interpreted . . . false interpretations appear as true . . . always religion's dilemmas. Beyond this, there are subconscious and superconscious views with far greater clarity. The sub and superconscious never work in words . . . they work exclusively in symbols and converse in symbolic language. As masters go deep into meditations of 'dhyana', they receive these information symbols. When written down, they're open to interpretation, but in the beginning they were accurately taught through oral traditions . . . no room for interpretations. Our prayer is that you allow the symbology of your life to come into your life without the need to interpret it . . . without the two dimensions of logic; that you allow this experience to remain in its magical dimensions without requiring it to identify itself with facts. Experience the harmony through which these symbols relate to the symbols of others . . . this is the root and the route of real peace.

*F*or real discovery to take place; for actual progress to be achieved on Earth; for true safeguards of harmonic living to be the new norm in this planet's movement to the future -- as Jesus, Muhammad, Einstein, Tesla, Nanak and the Buddha, amongst many, so clearly understood -- there needs to be a collective and connected director . . . like the director of an orchestra. This director is actually the human higher consciousness, for what's capable of accessing your higher consciousness, is also able to harmonize these disparate components; it coordinates the collective human awareness like a symphony. Human beings, more than any other creature, are constantly playing in the winds of change, and this is an important play of progress, but it's not without a severe downside. The directions of the winds of change are unpredictable, and when you get a hint of this limitlessness, that you're not bound, that there's total freedom everywhere, your responsibility must shift. You can no longer be selfish; no longer blame anyone, or hold them responsible for who, what, why, or when things are. There can be no complaining about the directions of the wind. This is the 'junction in crisis' that this world is challenged by in this very moment of evolution . . . it's the clock of the long now nearing midnight if you're not careful. This is where imagination comes into play. A moment like right now -- where there's little hope to be found in three and four dimensions -- is the best stimulant for imagination. This level of hopelessness is the birthplace for great ideas and ideals at the portal of greater dimensions. To pass through this "portal" is essential in times of darkness; to be on top of the "mountain" and see greater distances; to ride the "wave" of time without struggle as your awareness rises into higher consciousness is key. Our prayer is that you ride these winds of great change on the sails of your imagination; that you experience the sensations of limitlessness without blaming, or challenging the unfamiliarity, and then use these unfamiliar abilities to navigate the new course . . . become a director of harmony while the orchestra plays on.

*E*xistence is motion, right down to the particles within the atoms there's constant motion. Motion maintains location at every moment . . . this allows an identity to unfold its purpose. This is natural and meaningful, but also a problem. All this identity and purpose stirs up attachment to identity and purpose, which then produces conflicting identities and cross-purposes . . . the natural and essential often becomes violent. Non-motion -- beyond this three and four dimensional nature isn't limited, identified, or experienced by the senses. This is absolute clarity, but when in it, existence cannot be influenced. Like the clarity of a pond before motion stirs up the silt, this is the nature of total calm. The key is in the balance of purpose and calm . . . this creates benevolent influence. Crystal is the root of the word Christ; the root of Krishna . . . it is absolute clarity. When you are this clear, the physical, emotional, and psychological bodies have no blockages . . . they serve as a lens for the light body. In this way you're no longer limited inside three and four dimensions to a single location, or a single moment; you're free to explore the cosmos beyond the challenges of time, to locate their matching solutions, explanations and answers. This is the nature of your awakening; it's the ultimate purpose of your life in the human form. Your light-body's mission is an ancient code contained within the combinations and permutations of your genealogy and cosmology . . . your ancestry and your incarnations. Your light-body's mission is to solve the dilemmas found in this world of your time and space . . . this is your puzzle . . . you're the un-puzzler. As Lord Krishna said to Arjuna, "You knew what you'd face here on Earth, before you ever came to this Earth." In order to rise into this awareness of clarity, you must transform into your higher character through the dilemmas of these Earthly pressures. Our prayer is that you apply yourself daily -- with absolutely everything you do -- to create a personal practice to become that Christ; to become that Krishna; to become that crystal-clarity, and spread light into the darkness of these darkest of times.

The extinction of anything is devastating to everything. To develop higher consciousness; to achieve your highest awareness; to perceive the core connections of everything, everywhere -- is a journey that travels through millions of incarnations; experiences existences at countless levels, all to find the reason for life in every form. Just as beauty is in the eyes of the beholder, the reason for existence is found in the experience of existence . . . the reason for living is within the life that's alive. Your consciousness journeys through millions of possibilities of life -- all to gain a sensitivity; a perspective, and the acceptance of all life. There's an authority that's achieved at the end of this journey; an authority that allows you to track the history of your experiences and find inspiration. This authority comprehends the purpose of diversity, and the connections in polarity . . . it provides true guidance in every moment. This is the authority of compassion . . . the ability to experience the experience of another's existence at the moment of their experience. This authority arrives because you've been there . . . you've been everywhere. Raising your consciousness allows access to this vast memory, and to experience another's experience. To experience another's experience brings immediate recognition, instant connection with peace and love. This peace, connection and love -- over time -- allows sharing to spread abundance and prosperity. This is why the extinction of anything is so devastating to everything. It removes an entire series of experiences, erases angles of recognition, and once any of this is extinguished from possibility, the ability is gone from history. At a quantum level -- near the level of the soul -- time is just a perspective . . . it's not real. What happens in this moment, happens in every moment, and that which is gone from now, is simultaneously gone from forever . . . as if it never existed. The experience gained is erased. With every extinction, everything loses. Our prayer is that you understand the intricate reasons for all life; that you champion preservation, and inspire it with compassion.

*E*tymology -- the construction of words -- is a key to understanding human consciousness. Every word -- like ancient temples -- arose from the simple to complex utterances . . . sounds. Mantras . . . 'man' means both 'mind' and 'now' . . . 'tra' means 'projection' and 'acceptance'. The word confidence is 'con' plus 'fidence'. 'Fidence' is 'faith' and 'con' is 'with'. To be 'with faith' is confidence. Confidence locates skills in the darkness to generate light. This was always a capacity of the 'elite' . . . those who possessed the 'light' of 'El'. The Egyptian word for Saturn was El, and in the ancient teachings from Egypt, to India, to China, it was the 'Saturn' teacher who was always the elite teacher . . . the teacher with the light of El. Words with profound meanings trigger feelings and emotions. Emotions generate and secrete hormones from the glands and organs. Every person has the entire emotional "body" . . . every person has all of the emotions. Words are language -- the 'gauge' of 'length/depth' -- they activate emotions and give advantages, or disadvantages to life. Vantage is an extra view . . . the ability to see beyond. Anger, for example, is actually an angle of your vantage within a moment. It's most useful when it connects firmly to the moment and becomes determination -- to be undeterred. Determination is 'de' – another word for 'of' . . . 'termination' meaning the 'end' or 'outcome'. Determination is to be the outcome . . . to know the outcome. This was also called entitled -- those who had 'title' . . . those with advantage . . . the greatest 'vantage' or perspective. This was originally the condition of those who had awakened the Kundalini; who saw beyond the moment. These were the 'rulers' . . . rulers measure . . . and are to be measured up to. Rulers today are not rulers . . . to be measured up to; are not elite . . . of the light; are not confident . . . possessing faith, but are arrogant, and corrupted by false power. Our prayer is that you see yourself as elite . . . of the light; that you're entitled as a ruler to be measured up to; that you're a guide for life with confidence, and give the advantage of great vision to everyone now.

*L*ight travels in two forms -- particles and waves. Light particles are invisible, but the waves strike and reflect off material objects as the color and objects you see. Light travels longer distances primarily in particle form and becomes visible waves when observed nearby. These light particles carry limitless information throughout the entire Universe, Megaverse and Multiverse. This information requires order and meaning to be of value. Your consciousness assembles light particles -- known as photons either positive or negative in their charge -- in strings of meaningful code based on the arrangement of these charges. Your consciousness takes the invisible light and assembles thoughts and feelings . . . then interprets what they mean. When you're doing this in a highly conscious and accurate way, this is known as activating your 'light-body', or enlightenment. It's filled with intuition and innovation. Living bodies have significant amounts of light-carrying micro-crystals found in the fluids . . . human bodies are seventy percent water. These crystals are the salts, sugars, DNA, and various other types of mineral-crystalline compounds. Human consciousness creates meaning from this code by disciplining the 'light-body' with yoga and meditation; healthy food choices and diet, and many other forms of discipline. Activation creates calm and peace, but it's not initiated by calm and peace. Calm and peace don't stimulate, they sedate, and for activation there must be stimulation. The level of stimulation will determine the level of activation . . . the amount of activation determines innovation. Life on Earth right now is in an exponential state of existential crisis with huge innovation required. The stimulation has arrived at your doorstep in the form of new "leadership" in complete ignorance, and total denial. Our prayer is that you understand the nature and reason for this complete lack of leadership; that you use this stimulation to counter the disinformation contained in its darkness; activate your light-body as a leader with healthy practices, and use the fiasco of these times to ignite your light-body's mission.

With this current wave of global political anger, there's a rise of industrial denialism, an un-evolved collective consciousness that's ignoring the truth of this moment, while blaming the symptoms on unrelated reasons for economic benefit. Throughout the vast history of life, this mimics the signature habits of every lifeform that's ever gone into extinction. The early effects of this un-evolved denialism are already in motion as sea levels rise -- soon to increase exponentially -- all a result of the rapidly melting Greenland, Arctic, and Antarctic glaciers. The ultimate results of this denialism will occur as every coastal city goes under. Bangladesh, India, Pakistan, Southeast Asia, and Polynesia already see millions abandoning their homes, lands, and lives as the sea rises. The migration crisis, massive by today's view, will be just one global aspect in a new geological era -- the Anthropocene era -- catastrophic transformation of the world by human activity. The most important question in human history is upon you . . . "Will you survive beyond this un-evolved industrial denial?" There's comfort in relating to the absolute balance in the Cosmos at moments such as this . . . that in the darkness of ignorance and denial, there is always an equalizer . . . there by the laws of physics and nature. This balance is the massive light that must occur amongst this massive darkness . . . it must be summand however, physically and psycho-emotionally. In normal reaction mode, survival doesn't see this light in the treachery of darkness -- the fixation is on the darkness -- which is dangerous and captures the attention. It's time to lose this fixation; to get over the emotions of loss; to fulfill your proper course of grieving and mourning, but then put it to rest . . . completely. Give your-self a flexible point of reference to stimulate your progress for absorbing light. Our prayer is that you imagine realizations that will come with this light in the world; that you realize, with dark-ness, the largest light ever is there to discover all the evolutionary advancements required to avoid this disaster. Be a catalyst for sav-ing life . . . be a 'light-savior'.

Think of this largest moon in the context of the cosmic play, where there's nothing but perfect balance, and perfect balance produces perfect stasis . . . the calm depths that would ultimately become stagnation. As the world slides further into darkness, realize that exaggerated darkness breaks all the cosmic laws of balance, and when these laws are broken, evolutionary progress is triggered to rise out of its stagnation. This is what's happening in this very moment, and it will get even more profound . . . some of the most liberating pain ever will release you into the wild. And whenever a wild animal, which you're now becoming, gets cornered, it becomes its strongest. The current swarm of darkness is not just registering in your psyche; it's not just registering in your emotions, it's registering in your DNA, because the consequences of this dark unconsciousness is threatening all life on Earth. Get in touch with the animals and the wild animals; get in touch with the plants; get in touch with your own genetics; get in touch with your ancestors; get in touch with all of this and it will give you the accumulative strength to uncover deep answers; to manifest solutions; to be the antithesis and the antidote to the darkness that's swarming everywhere. For in the midst of all the darkness and danger of these times, and the coming times, you'll feel the greatest pressure mixed with your greatest strength . . . your wildness. In the midst of the natural doubts that accompany this awareness of massive strength, you might be tempted to ask the 'self-distracting' question, "Don't they know better?" Rest assured, the answer is a resounding NO. There's no way they can know better . . . they're not evolved enough to know better; they're not prepared enough to know better; they can't see over the fence of time far enough -- not even on their tiptoes -- to know better. Ignorance is at times an absolute blackout, and this is one of those times. Our prayer is that you embrace your wild; that you inhale your deep strength; wrap your arms around all that it exposes; find the hidden solutions in these disbelieving times . . . believe you're a savior, a prophet, a master, and don't expect to fit in.

There are many times throughout life when you're inspired to be your best, but it's rare in history when life is required to be its best . . . where there are no options -- you're either at your best -- or it's over. Such times are known as cataclysmic-evolutionary-catalysts (CEC), moments in the evolution of matter and life when options aren't available and the magnitude of change is both unimaginable and essential. Now is such a time -- the extreme agony that accompanies this moment has stripped away all freedoms of choice . . . your only choices are to be your very best, or there'll be no rest. Today there's a necessity of human leadership -- a 'future-proofing' of the planet -- an insuring there'll be life on Earth for a future to exist. The adolescents of evolutionary under-development have wrestled their way into all the positions of power; democracy has devolved into a mob rule; the epic quest for 'Lord of the Rings' has dissolved into the chaos of 'Lord of the Flies'. These are the darkest of times where medicines for profit have more side effects than benefits; where banking is not financial security, but a chop-shop of money gangsters; where industry has stopped making life better on Earth and is destroying life on Earth. And government, sweet government, is now an accumulator of lawless characters housed in an institution of anarchy. Within this ridiculous riddle -- in a world turned upside down -- you're on an assignment from Spirit, and have no choice. Either wake up, stand up, and show up, all the way up, or pack it up. At the threshold of human extinction, if you're paying attention, your awareness is agony set in treachery -- it's experiencing disloyalty causing great misery, and with no place to hide or run . . . no free will . . . you've got to be willing. Our prayer is that you experience this catastrophe and then resolve your honest mourning . . . it's a natural response; that you then bring yourself to the threshold of deep breaths each morning; set yourself into outstanding mode every day, and stand out in the crowds of your life, with the best possible performance of your life, for life depends on it . . . and on you . . . this is real.

*P*ain and fear are part of being aware, sensitive and empathic. It's a responsibility that comes with advanced human life . . . responsibility (the ability to respond) experiences this pain and the fear in full. They're the catalysts whenever there's a need for considerable change. If you're in pain and afraid right now, you have the empathic awareness to make a difference; you have this advanced ability to respond; you're one of a community who's on Earth to make a difference . . . the pain and fear are your guides. The Buddha said, "Any pain experienced to its core, turns to joy." The problem over millennia of human evolution is that pain was ignored, distracted, and numbed. Just like in natural childbirth, the pain guides your response . . . as the mother, you have this ability, for otherwise you'd not be pregnant. In the magic of re-creation, even the creation of new life, it's this awareness and presence that delivers the substance of the future . . . at the deepest levels of genetic reproduction it's the awareness of identity that magically recreates itself. The opportunity within your pain and fear is an obligation to use this advanced awareness; to recognize the opportunity within the darkness and respond to the ignorance (the ignoring of dangers). Turn up your light to such a degree that there's no denying reality. The darkness is scary because it's thought to be aggressive, but it's not aggressive, it's lacking light. It's the imagination in the darkness that's scary, but imagination can also be creative. Einstein said, "Imagination today is reality tomorrow." When the darkness is prevalent, as it is in this moment, your responsibility is your ability to respond -- to imagine the solutions in the pain, they're always there; to imagine what's being born through the pain, it's the contractions of labor; to imagine creating the change you want to see in the world, it's ready for activation with light. Our prayer is that you remember -- for every action, there's equal reaction; for all the current ignorance, there's equal awareness . . . the awareness is with you; the pain is your proof . . . be responsible . . . get active . . . imagine.

There's a unique sound and rhythm to your existence; your heart mimics this tone, beat and pulse . . . your heart is unique. Throughout the multiverse there's great light, and great darkness . . . your uniqueness has experienced them all . . . countless times. The current time is foretold in the Bible, the Torah, the Koran and the Vedas . . . every path forecasts this moment of now. Each time you've experienced lightness and darkness, you've been cutting a facet in the diamond of your existence . . . not a sensory experience of your existence, but the very core of the momentum within your moments . . . the vibrations within the particles within the parts. Just as your DNA markers are unique; your fingerprints are unique; your iris print is unique, and the print of your voice pattern is unique . . . the print of your heart's tone, pulse and beat is fully yours, and only yours. It experiences this darkness with the will to correct it . . . to light the way. You've been assigned to this darkness on this planet of your life, in this time of your life, for the sake of the planet's life. It's a moment to experience the difference and make a difference. When time is dark, you're here to be light, and in the moments of light, you're here to enjoy. In the face of the current danger and darkness, you're a warrior of accuracy, not violence. In the face of the current ignorance and folly, you're a scholar without judgement. In the face of the joy and light at the core of your being, remind yourself of who you are being. For you're a master and a prophet in a world of greed for profit; you're the bearer of miracles and masterpieces and it's time to stop performing them in the backyard of your life . . . move out onto this world stage of making a difference. You're not alone, it's a giant game of tag. Our prayer is that you know both you and the darkness are here for a reason; that you know in great risk, your faith is deeper; when your faith is deep, your prayer is louder; when your prayer is loud, the angels show up. Enter the risk on this Earth as a warrior; bask in the joy of your 'self' as a lover, and show up in these times of darkness as a savior . . . tag . . . you're it.

There's a responsibility in being human, and a greater responsibility when being a conscious compassionate one. This in itself demonstrates there's different levels of human development, just as there are different grades in a one-room schoolhouse. Your life is not a 'one-off' -- it's a progression throughout the multiverse, over countless star-systems, using millions of incarnations to achieve ultimate mastery . . . the final tens of thousands in human form. Not all humans have evolved to the level of demonstrating loving kindness in response to their challenges . . . some are just learning to crawl through time; others are learning to walk, or run over others, and a few have entered higher consciousness with the tools of empathy and compassion. Remember, Earth's a one room schoolhouse. The ratios from undeveloped to highly conscious are staggering, and the temptation is daunting for those who've progressed, to not feel superior. Throughout history there's examples of complete failures here . . . the consequences were dramatic. The caste system of India is a perfect example of complete failure amongst the highly conscious. What's speaking louder on Earth at this time is not the consciousness of people, what's loudest is the fear and insecurity; the survival of beliefs, of even genetic traits like skin-tone . . . all seem "important" to the undeveloped consciousness. Today's a perfect storm of phobia, bigotry and unconscious chaos. It's the time to look at this bigotry; to examine these phobias; to understand the insecurities that are causing this failure in human nature . . . to realize what's needed is a deep breath for yourself; a big hug for your highly conscious teammates; understanding -- without bias -- toward those less developed, and a strategy for creating a holism amongst the whole. Our prayer is that you sit in meditation within yourself; make a plan for yourself; create a 'dream-chart' of hopes and ways in which they'll be realized; become flexible with shifts and changes, for each breath delivers intuitive revelations . . . the game of life is in your hands . . . now you're the prophets . . . it's your time.

*T*hroughout material mechanics there's always a ratio of signal to noise, and the noise is consistently more prevalent than the signal. This is how matter operates. The purpose of individual human existence is to develop a consciousness that recognizes pure signals within this overwhelming noise. Throughout history there've been despotic individuals and movements, driven to find advantage in the noise; to appeal to the fear of noise, and then ride the waves of its storms to gain from its destruction. This is the nature of barbarism, a uniquely human condition influenced and organized by sociopathic inclinations . . . attitudes that have no empathy. This has become more prevalent since the ice ages destroyed the food-stocks and human ancestry defaulted to near-cannibalism. The ability to separate pure signals from overwhelming noise is the purpose of meditation, and at its highest levels, this awareness is known as awakening . . . as enlightenment. This is a specific capacity that empowers the electromagnetic field . . . your aura. The signal to noise ratio is like a needle in a haystack. There's a riddle: "How do you find a needle in a giant haystack? With a giant magnet!" When all the overwhelming noise registers on the sounding board of your life, the signal can be located by increasing your electromagnetic field to such a degree that you don't deal with the noise . . . it's noticed, but not engaged. You don't register it as value, but as an essential carrier-agent of the pure signals you attract. Evolutionary reality employs this signal to noise ratio to create environments of crisis; they stimulate growth, which enables change and adaptation to survive and thrive. Those who take advantage of the noise, for the purpose of self-gain, are servants of this evolutionary process . . . they stimulate those who are approaching enlightenment. Our prayer is that you're not discouraged by the noise, but see beyond these charades and parades to embrace the pure signals they contain . . . shed the noise and the antics of those who take advantage of destruction and recognize it's all part of cosmic nature . . . locate the signals and use them for good.

The ionosphere surrounding the Earth has a positive electrical charge; the Earth's surface carries a negative charge . . . this presents an electrical tension inside the space between the two fields . . . the 'Earth-Ionosphere-Cavity' - E.I.C. Two concentric polarity-charge balls -- one inside the other -- is an active capacitor. Between the Earth and the ionosphere there's a circulation of energy, like a life-force; there's a pulse and a frequency, like the heartbeat and breath; there's massive capacity for information transfer, like a nervous system . . . the Earth is alive and breathing in every sense of the concept. Nikola Tesla was the first to discover this powerful electro-magnetic circulating tension . . . it penetrates the Earth without resistance and thereby produces a resonance frequency known as the tone of the Earth. The Earth is a living event, just like you and every other plant and animal. In 1952 the German physicist Professor, William Schumann at the University of Munich, measured this resonance -- these electro-magnetic waves -- and found they have a frequency of 7.83 Hz. The Earth vibrates and makes the sound of this frequency, which happens to also be the gateway rate of the brain's dreamtime state, and of deep meditation. It's called the 'theta-state', and when you train your brain to operate at this frequency, you perceive far more information in every moment; you're not bound by the three and four dimensions of spacetime; your consciousness can travel beyond these limits and visit the history of the past -- which still vibrates -- and the history of the future -- which is already "written". This is where your consciousness resides, both in dreamtime and in deep vipassana meditation . . . the nature of your natural silence, where you can absorb nearly infinite information. This is the world of the higher consciousness, and the responsibility of all people who want to make a difference on this Earth. Our prayer is that you do the work to live at this frequency of the Earth's natural tone; that you use this level of consciousness to discover the answers and solutions for this moment in history . . . and eliminate all the troubling mysteries.

Synchronicity is not a miracle, nor an anomaly -- synchronicity runs parallel to chaos and overwhelm. Chaos and overwhelm are angles of perception -- distortions of the subatomic structure that's everywhere always. Synchronicity is continuously present . . . it's contained within the sense of presence. Humanity has left this sensation and awareness of presence behind for the past several hundred years. Ever since science and industry claimed they could control nature, the sense of a material world having powers beyond what can be measured has been passionately discounted. But synchronicity is actually at the base of what's being measured . . . it's the constant reliance on measuring that limits this awareness . . . synchronicity cannot be measured, and when you try to measure it . . . it disappears. Current life is being acted out on the "screen of this disappearance" . . . far from the realm of what is . . . it simply isn't. When life is synchronistic, you experience what is . . . things fall into place . . . the constant coincidences cause confidence . . . the confidence then allows you to experience gratitude as your normal state. In drifting away from this awareness, the normal state has become fearful not grateful -- there's strong longing for preference, but very little attempt at being present . . . it's considered too emotionally raw. When you're not present, and you're longing for preference -- you dwell in neither -- you live in the difference. This difference is a very painful place . . . home to the post-industrial human majority. This glitch in the current human psyche -- a trap outside of time -- tries to define and measure the time that isn't. You can overcome this overwhelming sense by breathing into a belief in synchronicity . . . breathing and believing that synchronicity is the more natural state. Our prayer is that you develop gratitude for what's taking place in your life; know that synchronicity is right there on a parallel track; take on the weight of that which you perceive . . . embrace the sensations of your breathing and the weight will pass right through you, revealing synchronicity as normal.

The many imbalances and disturbances that take place in the details of your life, allow for growth and movement to evolve within the perfect balance of the bigger picture. Perfect balances are static, they don't move, or allow for the unknowns of growth, but they're an essential environment for all life to exist and persist. The microcosmic revolutions that take place in the details within this stasis, produce revelatory shifts in the evolution of spacetime. The macrocosm is a 'holism' with a perfect balance and a constant synchronicity that coordinates everything with everything. Communication across this holism takes place at the instantaneous speed of thought. Within this total equilibrium -- your will, your intention, your motivation and inspiration are commanders of the movement if you choose to make it so. This movement is sometimes gentle and smooth, but it can also be chaordic or chaotic. It's of no value to complain or blame these disturbances of motion . . . it's up to you to establish a commanding authority amongst them. The [word] command refers to the two minds of all moments -- your finite human mind, and the infinite universal mind. Coordinating and cooperating these two minds is how your consciousness becomes relevant to the moment. Blameless connection with the engines of chaos -- the drivers of growth and change -- allows you to master chaotic life within the vast cosmic synchronicity . . . order within chaos within order. This command is extremely relevant -- it's the alchemy of your destiny that shapes the relationship between your human nature and a perfectly balanced cosmic nature. This creates natural growth, conscious growth, and evolutionary growth. Our prayer is that when your

world is challenging and chaotic, you take a moment to reconnect with the macrocosmic balance beyond it . . . imagine all
these disturbances demonstrating creativity and vital movement.
Shifting your awareness to this natural synchronicity, blesses these
imbalances and disturbances, for they are essential to growth, and
at the very heart of change.

*M*any years ago a student asked Yogi Bhajan, "Where will you be after you're gone?" He leaned into the students face and touched his nose to their nose and said, "Closer than this." There's a freedom that comes with liberation, a freedom that does not come with just death, but from completing the assignments of life. Without the body, and not needing to get into another, the tasks of an angel are the tasks of a liberated being. The goal of all life is to be liberated when you've completed it. Then you can be in multiple places at once; serve as many people as will accept your assistance; travel beyond the limits of sequenced time, and simply follow the thoughts of the Universal mind that are tuned to the quest of a liberated consciousness. This is the freedom of liberation; this is the goal of every life; this is the path of every dharma, and the result of all great disciplines. There's a sacred hymn that says, "Live such a life that has ever been lived, so you won't have to die again." Each time you leave your body behind, you're greeted by the most perfect version of you . . . this is your full mirror. The degree to which you can see yourself in this vision and version is the degree of your liberation . . . this is the true nature of forgiveness -- 'giving yourself forward' -- to match the most perfect you. During life, these three and four dimensions of spacetime are a practice field for this timeless and space-less moment . . . the opportunity to participate in observing yourself with equanimity and perfect benevolence. Since the ultimate reality is that the observed and the observer are the same event, the only question is -- how long will it take for you to commit your Earthly reality to this Universal principle? When will your senses connect to the oneness of everything? Our prayer is that you sense your greatest self in the hint of every moment that you experience; that you accept the help of the angels that are closer to you now than they were in life; that you dedicate your days to your liberation and the liberation of others, and that you live a life of service so that liberation comes naturally when all your days are done.

*A*ll that has already happened in the world -- the light and sound vibrations of all events -- is still in motion across the universe, and will be in motion until the momentum is released. Even the momentum in your DNA lasts for seven generations . . . this is two hundred and fifty four ancestors who are influencing you. This is the continuation of their epigenetic momentum living out through your thoughts and feelings. Such is the continuum of the past, and there's also a continuum of the future . . . all that's yet to happen already exists as a vibrational distribution of the parts . . . waiting for the 'confluence' to assemble the future of now. Having foreknowledge is intuition . . . the clear view of all the inclinations existing amongst these parts that assemble the future. This accumulation contains tipping points that trigger the inclinations of this distribution and assemble the exact result. When you trace back from any point in this process, you realize everything that's going to be, already exists . . . just not yet assembled. When you reach out beyond the limited appearance of time, you enter the momentum of this assembling assemblage. A single sequence of time displays limitations, but this is only a portion of the total. When your awareness stretches beyond this sequence and into the entire consequence -- and you do this with benevolence -- the entire assemblage will appear in all the possible forms for your influence on the confluence. This is true alchemy. You're able to influence this world of three and four dimensions of spacetime with benevolent intentions. It's a reflection, deflection, and refraction within this intentional process . . . a consequence of every other moment in time. All the waves that were ever produced, affecting every other moment that will ever exist. Our prayer is that you're aware of these continuous connections and use them to achieve benevolent goals; that you work with the waves of momentum to accumulate better moments; that through your faith and hope you expose the joy that's a part of all times, and that you breathe prosperity into the needs of those less fortunate all over the world.

With a powerful enough telescope, you can see as far into the space of space as millions and billions of light years away. The light you're seeing in these images come from star systems that may have been born, lived, and have already died all before you're seeing them. Imagine another capacity: you have an even more powerful telescope within your own brain; you can see not only the star-systems at great distance, but you can see down into the planets within these systems, and the even lives of the beings that are living on these planets . . . certainly in a multiverse as large as 'near-infinity' you don't believe you're the only ones. So you're viewing the moments in these lives that have taken place thousands, millions, even billions of years ago and you're viewing it as if it's in the present tense . . . interacting with this view would be interacting with that which was. Now imagine further . . . since there's always a reaction that's equal to every action, it's therefore possible that you're also able to act with lives in the future . . . the light, by the way, is always there. So now you must ask yourself, "Why do you limit the view of life that you interact with; why do you believe any of the limitations that you believe in; how can you break the spell and capture the wealth from the past, and the future, for the presentation of your presence?" This is the great quest of all the questions that have stimulated consciousness forever. To become that which you are to be, you must accept that this is what you've always been. This is the nature of your destiny; this is the nature of your capacity; this is the nature of your projection throughout spirit when you release any sense that you are "desperate" . . . meaning without spirit. Our prayer is that you look out through "time" and visualize that you are right on time; that you look out through time and realize it's your time to be everything imaginable; that you look out through time and give yourself the authority to have the time of your life with the time of your life . . . for it's always all yours forever.

*A*mongst human beings, there's rarely a pure sense of how things truly are; of what's actually taking place in any given moment. This is the rare state of conscious mastery . . . the awakening that the great masters experienced throughout time. There's an innate human ability however, to connect in this way to the source, to experience the origins of where everything comes from, but it's rare for anyone to experience this ability. Instead, humanity is mostly attempting to reconcile their fears, doubts and concerns. There's a very old saying amongst the awakened ones -- "That which you don't embrace, you'll have to face until you do." In other words, when you set something up in your fears and doubts -- when you avoid connecting because of your emotional blockages -- you'll have to face it in some form and embrace it in order to resolve the fears and doubts that separate you from the moment. Having the ability to experience the world at its source delivers an understanding of how each moment arrives at this moment. This is what's called, "experiencing the way it is." This ability to see the source is what was known as a source-seer . . . [sorcerer] in modern language. This was the original teachings of all the great religions -- the prophets would teach what they themselves had mastered, and the followers would become as adept as the prophet . . . they were called "Adepts". Even the name religion, comes from the conjoining of the two words [realize-origin] . . . to realize and recognize the origin or source. Over time, the competitive emotions spread amongst the practitioners, and then, to reduce this conflict, the religious systems turned toward only worshipping the prophet and withholding the teachings. Our prayer is that you're determined to become a master in your own right, and know that you have this right; that you use all the great disciplines and technologies to experience yourself; to recognize yourself; to become as great as anyone who's ever lived; to discipline your life as a disciple and experience reality . . . to have the pure sense of how things truly are.

The path of benevolent mediation is a path in which the angles of your values are consistent to triangles of the resistance. Establishing the outcomes of your desires, without specific attachment to these definitions, is a means of travelling with your relationships through the spaces within the possibilities, toward the times that are provided. The result is right there, and it's always fair . . . this is the law of physics. To use these guaranteed channels in guiding your trajectory through time, is to use the nourished spaces that guide and nourish all sides of life's equation. Sit and listen for the "right" motion in the midst of each silent moment; trust the presence of this motion when it presents itself; use this presence to achieve a desired mutuality, and mediation will complete itself without competing with itself. This is the mediation that carries you through the maze of life . . . it's the guarantee that infinity uses to enable life's relations. A wise master once said, "Never be amazed . . . it only verifies your disbeliefs." As the prefix "a" indicates "without" . . . 'a-maze-ing' means being without the maze -- the illusion -- that everyone's normally experiencing. And because the path of right mediation is also the path to your destination, there's nothing amazing about it . . . just the reality of a "river". A "river" may not always be flowing directly toward the sea, but nevertheless, the river is always going to the sea. The rivers of the world are all heading to the ultimate destination of the oceans of the world, but they must twist and turn through the hills and valleys in order to get there. When you finally arrive at the ocean of your life, whenever and whatever this is, to be amazed would mean that you were not knowing that this was -- by cosmic law -- going to take place. And in the larger picture, you're always there. Our prayer is that your meditations on your mediations in life are ones that recognize this guarantee; that you live with the faith that every moment connects to your destiny; that this produces the connections you appreciate with your life, and the result is a benevolence that surrounds you at all times.

The human sensory memory retains an exact copy of what's being seen, heard, touched, tasted, and smelled . . . this registers as events described as space within moments of experienced time. Time is a wave connecting the various points of space . . . a continuous pattern that allows matter and energy to play out their collective natures of existence within your perceptions. In this particular star-system, all of this matter comes from the Sun . . . as its energy of light travels to Earth and other celestial bodies. When this reaches its destination, it returns to matter . . . then within the embrace of this destination it turns into the energy of life . . . everything is alive. This is a constant cycle throughout the universe; the megaverse; the multiverse. It's been recycling for millions, billions, trillions, quadrillions, and beyond when measured in Earth years, though measuring is an ironic concept when relating to such a seemingly endless accumulation. As vast as this is however, it's but a blink in the eye of what many refer to as GOD . . . just a blink. Each of these blinks has an individual destiny to be fulfilled, and when you're riding the waves within its space, you're acting out your destiny within another destiny . . . the coincidental fulfillment of destinies. Within this collective interaction is born the existence of you as you, a gifted number of breaths to experience your sensory memory . . . all the time your spirit knowing this definition is an illusion, within an illusion using the count of your breaths for the process. No one remains when the count of their breaths is complete, and no one leaves until this is done. Earth's atmosphere is filled with these spirits all counting . . . the atmosphere is in fact the "Atma sphere" . . . the sphere of recycling Atmas. Our prayer is that you engage this energy and matter with the fullness of your spirit, and make life matter with your energy; that you use your senses to register all that's experienced by your breaths in each moment, and then deliver to this star-system the greatest blessings you can project from the light you've received . . . be a lighthouse for all your relation-ships.

The numbers of the wild animals roaming this Earth is essential to the ecosystem, the bio-system, and incarnation's evolutionary system. It's already failing and set to fail by even more horrendous numbers very soon. From the global count in 1970, it will fall by two-thirds when the calendar arrives at 2020. You are personally participating in a mass extinction that's destroying the natural world upon which you depend. The analysis, the most comprehensive to date, indicates that animal populations have currently plummeted by fifty-eight percent from 1970 to 2012, and are now on track to reach sixty-seven percent destruction by 2020. This research was done by the World Wildlife Fund and the Zoological Society of London . . . the scientific study found that the destruction of wild habitats; hunting/poaching/fishing, along with air, water and land pollution were to blame . . . all of this is man-made. This is a revelation that's beyond just the campaigns of concerned organizations to resolve . . . this is universally personal, and globally imminent. This revelation requires a wholesale shift in the collective human consciousness, and the only way to approach such a catastrophic event is by setting an impersonally personal example . . . by communicating with every breath, and every action you take. This is a challenge to the cultures of this world; to the corporations of the world; a challenge to every individual on the Earth. The only way to meet such a challenge is to reach out and teach out through every relationship you own . . . "tag, you're it". Our prayer is that you're completely unwilling to sit back and allow this to happen on your watch; that you're going to make this realization a part of your conscious existence with every breath . . . every moment; that you realize you're an active part of this problem if you're not an active ingredient in the solution . . . and with every part of your ego (bigger the better); every part of your physiology and psychology ("crazier" the better), you decide to be a "savior" (one amongst many) that this planet has been waiting for . . . for a very long time. "Tag . . . you're it."

Synchronicity is miracle based living. In the vast and endless expanses of the cosmos, infinite proximity is the quantum reality that keeps life evolving. This infinite proximity produces an extraordinarily exact mimicry throughout the various star systems; maintains an evolutionary clarity, and allows your incarnations to take place anywhere throughout the universe; the megaverse, and if you're truly advanced, anywhere throughout the multiverse. Einstein called this the "theory" of twin particles -- but it's a "theory" in name only, because it is, in fact, a pure reality . . . a cosmic law. This is the perfect communication -- not limited by any mega-amount of space or time -- that allows your incarnations to take place in one galaxy or universe, and then pick up in subsequent incarnations in another galaxy, or another universe, or even beyond this measure the next time around . . . all without the slightest flaw. This exact mimicry produces the realization of invariable synchronicity . . . miracle-based living . . . the condition of your 'spirit' being in constant union with the universal 'soul' . . . the dance of Atma (individual spirit) and Paramatma (universal soul). Your higher consciousness is always aware of this harmonic dance; tuning in to this with your consciousness allows you to enjoy its coordination, cooperation, and phenomenal comforts within every experience of your daily life. It puts the prayer of the Buddha into perfect action . . . "Wherever you are to be, you shall be; whoever you are to meet, you shall meet; whatever you're to say, you shall say, and what you are to accomplish, is already done." The star-system in which your life is currently being lived greets you with your accumulative destiny as a gift of fulfillment. All of this is pre-programmed into your DNA with the excitatory neurons targeting postsynaptic neurons and glandular cells to cause your thoughts and feelings to unfold as guides . . . rather than disruptions or disturbances. Our prayer is that you accept this gift of synchronicity from the infinite grace, and live with it as your lifestyle and life-cycle . . . a perfect guidance system.

*C*onscious growth lies in the unknown, that which is there for you, but not yet known to you. It's courage that permits you to explore this great region of both the actual and virtual worlds. The word courage means "a time of the heart" -- where 'cour' means 'heart', and 'age' means 'the time'. This time of the heart allows you to explore the unknown, and as you grow into it, you make it known. This is inspiration . . . courage transforming unknowns into safe zones. The dichotomy is, until you feel safe, your heart is closed -- when you feel safe, your heart opens up . . . when your heart opens, you feel safe. This cycle of higher consciousness requires a spark to light it . . . this spark is faith . . . leaping into this unknown. Unlike a vicious cycle -- this courageous cycle holds the keys to your future. Faith allows you to move forward through inspiration . . . the vicious cycle of fear freezes you in the known past. There's an 'interactive-mind' and a 'universal-mind'. The 'interactive-mind' -- accessed through your head-brain -- is the collection of memories and opinions . . . the known territories of the old all jumbled together. With this mind running your life, there's zero inspiration from achieving anything new. This mind fills time with attractive distractions; being busy protecting territories, but never exploring the unknown. This is modern humanity descending into territorial protection, corruption, violence, war and terror. On the other side there's the 'universal-mind' -- accessed through the heart – it's a collection of everything that's never been known; inspiration from achieving something new and compelling; the transformation of uncertainty that comes from conscious growth. In the midst of all this -- in the environments explored with your open heart -- you're driven by caring for others not competing with them . . . your breath plants the seeds for a future of mutual benefit. Our prayer is that you take these leaps of faith; that you create through inspiration and open your heart with courage; that you establish a new evolution of conscious growth, and set this as your example for others to follow.

In every moment of psycho-emotional slavery -- the inability to resist thoughts and feelings from controlling life -- there's a parallel version running free and unnoticed alongside this experience. Parallel to every moment filled with worry -- without faith; afraid -- without trust, and littered with plans abandoned in doubt, there's the same plans awaiting fulfillment and success awaiting your experience . . . like an alternate universe, always right there. Being a slave to thoughts and feelings is normal, but when it intensifies, it is agony. Agony is an agent of great change . . . it is nature. Begin by realizing you're the one feeling your feelings . . . loosen their strength by becoming their witness. You can make choices as a witness . . . believe you can. First, be aware there's this parallelism . . . this opens the potential for its freedom. Second, believe you can step into it. Third, give yourself the authority to do so. Fourth, make your move on pure faith. This turns emotions and feelings into tools for life, not the rules for life. They're physically powerful and seem real, but they're only memories of human opinions all jumbled together in the 'interactive-mind'. Feelings are often parts of the shells that protect seeds . . . the seeds that contain dreams. Not to be owned as absolute commands, feelings are to be honed to take command of the seed. They're not to be obeyed, but until you break their spell, they'll assure you that they are. A carpenter doesn't obey the hammer -- the hammer is respected and used as a tool. The tools of feelings and thoughts are helpful -- at times essential -- they can build, and destroy your moments. Our prayer is that until you're their master, don't be their slave; that you take deep inhales through your nose and exhale through your mouth whenever these tools of your psycho-emotional body try to take over command; that you make a determination with your determination whenever there's anxiety, frustration, or anger . . . and allow the vision that comes with this breath, to expose the parallel version right alongside this moment . . . it's the version with momentum going forward in your dream.

*T*here's a meditative process -- practiced by yogis for thousands of years -- known (in English) as 'deep etheric lucid dreaming' (DELD). Lucid dreaming uses the theta-state (dream-state) of the brain while conscious. The world, as you experience it normally, is actually an assortment of attitudes, opinions and views, which work as filters attached to your senses, feelings and 'emotional memory' . . . emotions distort this moment from previous moments. D.E.L.D. allows the brain to capture screens of your reticular memory -- ancient notes from your incarnate past -- held as vital instincts in the brain's reticular activating system (RAS). This consciousness of the ancient memory, can guide you through the lessons of this lifetime, by using the essence of what's already been mastered. Because the RAS is awake during sleep, it's a perfect avenue for lucid dreaming to access this core of your filters that hold the emotional keys. This meditation is a deep visualization process that travels through millions of incarnations . . . just the visual essence . . . none of the details. By descending through this matrix of natural imagery, you use ancient essences to activate current neurons in the brain's limbic "classifier". This meditation changes the endocrine "conversations" going on throughout your limbic system -- you optimize your current "dream", through a collective awareness of your ancient past. Real changes result in your 'stimulus-response' mechanics. This is how great masters pass through their moments so easily . . . with all these emotional filters at their command, they turn them off, and pass through the "what is" -- instead of wrestling with the "what is appearing" -- always distorted by the filters of emotional memory. In other words, they experience the reality of each moment, without maya distorting it from history. Our prayer is that you begin this meditative process through daily yoga, deep breathing, and forgiveness; that you prepare the ground for the present moment, using gratitude from your deep collective past, and that you open the doors to a limitless future within this moment.

*T*ime is the illusion of recordings, constructed in the brain-mind connection, from memories that generate anticipations. The shift between memories and anticipations creates a sensation of motion . . . this sensation is experienced as passage of time through moments. The stronger this sense of passage is -- the more momentum is contained in the motion. It's a tool that the brain-mind connection uses to keep track of life: a series of memories plus anticipations -- assembled as a means of building one upon another -- measuring goals that appear to be growing through these moments . . . moments appearing as real segments of life. Reality -- for what that's worth is: all time is a single unmeasurable moment, and all space is a single point of no dimension . . . a singularity. As described above, the brain-mind connection slices and sequences this singularity to make it measurable. Within these sequences -- known as maya -- every moment is a seed. And like the seeds of a great tree -- each one contains every branch, leaf, flower, fruit and seed for every year that the tree shall live through . . . plus every future tree that will come from each new seed. Every bit of this infinite cycle exists inside every seed. Time is a seed, an infinity of moments packed into a shell of protection . . . all the future moments exactly replicating memories of the past . . . all the branches, leaves, flowers, berries, and more seeds. Your life, and more, is contained within each seed of your time; each moment is filled with goals -- like branches, leaves and fruit -- filled with infinite possibilities. You can nourish and water them with faith and hope, or waste and starve them with confusion and doubt. Time -- the illusion of moments -- is the greatest measuring invention your life has to offer when you use it . . . and when you don't, it's an agony beyond measure. Our prayer is that you'll allow yourself to open the unknown doors of infinite time; don't ask how, just determine that you will because you can . . . and in this process, create the time of your life with the time of your life . . . it's all up to you in each moment . . . use relentless discipline for mastery . . . do it.

*Y*our consciousness -- the spirit of individual existence -- attaches to the Soul which is universal to everyone. In Sanskrit, this is the Atma (individual) attached to Paramatma (universal). Higher consciousness is this individual spirit with a mission and purpose, and it dreams of this with the heart. Powered by the soul, your life seeks this awareness -- when it connects you discover 'destiny' . . . a life lived on purpose. Destiny can be shaped and molded by your commitment to this mission/purpose when the 'heart-brain' is leading. These are the choices you make with each breath you take . . . head or heart. The higher your existence becomes, the more your life must be led by the brain in your heart . . . it is evolution, but it's not without anguish. When you're about to grow into destiny, the brain in your head will appear like an enemy; make my life seem horrible; haunt you with neurotic inferences, and this is why the masters referred to it as the "monkey mind". It's no longer your main home . . . you've graduated to the higher reasoning of your heart-center. In this new state, you'll view life without filters; the 'maya' (illusion) fades . . . reality has no filters. Filters are like the training wheels on a bicycle, they assist in achieving balance, but once balance is achieved, they'll get in your way. You've spent lifetimes with the 'head-brain' leading, but once higher purpose has been touched, the 'heart-brain' must take the lead, with the 'head-brain' to follow. You'll notice in brief moments of heartfelt joy -- immediately the 'head-brain' discounts it with deep old-pattern thoughts . . . the jealousy of transition. It may seem quite different on Earth right now as the illusion is thick and distracting with sparkle and choices . . . the world still thinks its purpose is with the marketplace. Our prayer is that your heart takes the lead in your life; spend time each day breathing consciously into your heart and feed this graduation into purpose. At the core of your chest feel the force of each breath and feed your process of living on purpose, and when the "monkey" head goes crazy, embrace it . . . comfort it . . . it's just jealous . . . it's OK.

*T*here's an 'angle' through which you enter and exit any given moment -- it determines the amount of ease and grace, or challenge and struggle you experience in the moment. These 'angles' are composed in your brain's sense of time, and the body's sense of three dimensional space. Your life records and monitors these 'angles' using the fascia -- that webbed network traveling throughout your body -- wrapping the glands and organs . . . the ligaments, bones, tendons, and muscles, plus the extensions of the arms, legs, head and neck. All of this produces the information that your brain and body interpret as moments. These complex 'angles' are carried from lifetime to lifetime by your spirit; they come with your DNA at birth . . . their genetic origins dating back seven generations. They're also produced through your current experiences. Known as epigenetics, this large portion of your DNA is mutable. You're actually able to alter these 'angles' with your attitude . . . pull your brain out of its patterns . . . transform the inclinations of your thoughts and feelings, and create your own choices. The stronger the patterns embedded in the brain -- the stronger the raw material you have to work with -- but also -- the harder it is to work with them. This indicates an advanced capacity . . . a mastery for impacting the Earth . . . but the intensity is severe as well . . . the power is daunting. One day, in my personal agony and frustration, I questioned the master, Yogi Bhajan, "Why does this always have to be so difficult?" His answer was instant, and he delivered it with a smile, "GOD doesn't want jerks in Heaven," was all he said. And when -- in my irritated opinion -- I questioned the validity of this "smart-ass" answer . . .

he just said it again, eyes pointing directly at me. "GOD does not want . . . jerks in Heaven." Our prayer is when the patterns of your brain seem impossible; when all the moments of your life angle against you; when you long for relief from your thoughts and emotions . . . change the angles in your body; stretch into your body-glove; bolt your butt to the yoga mat and ride it till it surrenders . . . become the power of your awkward mastery till it's no longer awkward.

Today's world does not recognize the full power of half of the physical creation. This is the half that's based in the feminine. The women of the world at this time are tasked with the obligation to insist on this changing before it's too late. This is the base nature of the world's conflicts . . . even pollution is the negligence and disrespect for the mother . . . the Mother Earth. This disrespect of the feminine has been present for tens of thousands of years, but it's now becoming obvious and collectively painful. The portion of material physics that's obvious and predictable and measureable is logic. This (law-gic) makes laws. There's another half available and essential -- the half that has no obvious characteristics, but is equally as real. This is the magic half -- the "ma" -- the "mir" of miracle . . . the mother. It's unpredictable, unobservable, and unmeasurable, yet none of these characteristics create chaos. Chaos is a product of the logical brain's desire for measurement and predictability. Magic (miracles) happen when you release this logical desire to interfere with the infinite creativity. The miraculous ways of the feminine produce that which can then be logically measured. The current world -- the world of the patriarchy -- is obsessed with measurement and "law and order" -- and there must be a natural order, in order for lives to coexist. But there must also be the flexibility of disorder, in order for life to continue. Without creativity there's no evolution, and without evolution -- stagnation, pollution and corruption will dominate and destroy. Our prayer is to the mothers in everything; to the feminine part of everyone; to the part of you that is unmeasurable and beautifully unpredictable . . . set it free and insist on its freedom . . . let it be the joy that's at your core . . . let it create the future so that life can prosper . . . respect all women.

Seven million years ago your ancestors began standing -- it took four million years to master this balance, and from that moment to now, nature has been modifying human anatomy for one ultimate purpose . . . maximum awareness; processing subtle energy, and achieving enlightenment. You've arrived . . . you're crossing over from the old purpose of survival and aggression, to an entirely new era. All of the survival emotions based in fear are obsolete, but they're refusing to leave, and this is where evolution becomes dangerous. A two legged animal that's developed such magnificent intelligence, must discard its emotional insecurity, or it will destroy itself. Like a multi-stage rocket, if the previous stages remain attached, the whole journey will falter and fail. The new evolutionary intention, the one that's available if you're paying attention, is a world of innocent curiosity, with profoundly non-logical discoveries. It reaches beyond these three dimensions of space and the fourth dimension of time . . . it's not about territorial ownership of any kind . . . it's about sharing the commons . . . what's common to nurturing all life. The human child is born helpless and innocent, and takes longer to mature than any other species . . . these initial frailties cause all children to experience the worlds beyond this world, the worlds of awareness, creativity, and higher consciousness. Being born physically helpless, aides in this journey. Countless millions have used evolution for this new assignment, but their actions have been buried by the aggression of the masses who've not. History is always written by the "victors", and human history is littered with the stories of victorious aggression against far more conscious -- non-aggressive -- indigenous cultures. For eons humans have evolved these bodies for this moment in time to arrive. These bodies are now finely tuned instruments, completely prepared for the new voyage of the spirit. Our prayer is that you begin this voyage; that you use your body to explore its highest purpose; that you welcome the awareness that's already there . . . just waiting for you to take notice and share.

When obsession with image has become primary in human interaction, it stimulates the economy, but never embraces harmony . . . fixating on competition and comparison . . . pain is the natural result. The modern economy has been delegated to capitalizing on competition. "All is fair in love and war" . . . "The art of war" are acknowledged primers for "success". But life and living are not nourished in competition; the realization that life is a sacred gift, endowed to carry consciousness through a living experience does not have a need to compete. Your physical life is a transceiver: you transmit an image of physical light -- it reflects off everything and returns as the image of your environment. You live in this environment to achieve a realization of you. With this reflection in your senses -- you feel; you think, and you grow with "beauty being in your own eyes". Add the element of competition and comparison to this, and your life stops growing forward and runs in comparison-circles. This has been humanity's journey for the past thousand years . . . about to consume the planet beyond livability. For when life focuses on image, the physical world consumes to satisfy the high maintenance of insecurity . . . no time is left to nourish the consciousness . . . no sense of an ultimate fulfillment. Now is the time to account for life and determine how much is contracting with image. There's a mindset beyond image, an opportunity to connect -- to be mindful of your moments -- to tune the body instrument for supporting health . . . this will actually provide a profound image . . . the image of harmony. Our prayer is that you use your body to create a healing experience; that you release your 'self' from the collective slavery of image, and focus on the wisdom of connecting mind with body to achieve harmony. This focus enables real health and healing . . . the image that results is a revelation; a realization . . . the image of you being you is the most beautiful you.

It's said -- everyone wants change, but don't want it to be too different. Even though change is the only constant, change is also a considerable challenge to manage. In order create the change you desire; for [the] who you want to be; what you want to be; why you want to be, and when you want to be all of this . . . to actually take place . . . you must first embrace everything 'that is' right now. For it's within this embrace of 'what is' at any moment, that you're able to create an alliance with your subconscious -- the part of your mind that holds your world in place. With this alliance -- the aspects of your mind that are rigidly holding everything that's current -- open up to the possibility of shifting positions -- open up to consider releasing the inherent fear of the unknown -- thereby allowing insights of the new path to appear within the intuition . . . this is what hope is made from. When you don't accept the way things currently are, there's a gap in this alliance . . . a gap between the soul and the spirit -- the body, emotions, and the subconscious. In this gap there's complete disconnect -- a subconscious sense that you're the enemy . . . and hope fades. You merely experience a defiance . . . an identity that's not who you are, but who you're not . . . not what you want, but what you don't. Your desire (your preference) becomes your only reference point . . . you abandon the presence that you don't embrace -- yet it's your only connection to this moment -- and live in the pain of the gap. This difference is the spacetime that has no space, and is always out of time . . . it's in between your presence and your preference. But when you breathe deeply and reoccupy yourself fully -- it means you're embracing all that you are in this moment . . . both the presence and the preference . . . life will arrive to fulfill your desires with change. Our prayer is that you welcome the change of your preference by embracing the reality of your presence; that you long for the change that you live for, and live in the life that is here. In this way you'll enjoy and then change what you see in your world . . . in love with your space, and always on time.

GOD has been the topic of admiration, discussion, competition and war for thousands of years. GOD has been whatever a culture defined it as -- but oddly -- GOD cannot actually be defined by that which GOD created . . . nothing can define its maker. And this has been the challenge at the core of all disharmony and violence between humans without awareness. Yogi Bhajan teased that GOD was an acronym . . . G.enerates-O.ganizes-D.elivers. Synchronicity, conscious mimicry, parallel symmetry, and absolute identity are dance partners with this generating-organizing-delivering force . . . and to dance in this dance, is to live in a 'miracle-based' life. As the prayer of the Buddha said, "The places you are to be, you shall be; the people you're to meet, you shall meet; the words you're to speak, you shall speak, and the success you are to have, you shall have. When this synchronicity moves with such parallel symmetry, there's an equally conscious mimicry that delivers an absolute GOD-like identity, but with no idea of the true vastness that's involved. This is where heartfelt humility comes in, for with this process of GOD-like synchronicity, the focal-point of awareness must move from being exclusively with the brain, to being balanced . . . primarily with the heart, and yet extremely inclusive of the brain. It moves from intellect alone, to an intuitive-wisdom where synchronicity -- with all of its conscious mimicry, parallel symmetry, and absolute identity resides. This is living a miracle-based life; this is being the change you want to see in the world. This is the path of time that produces the changes you choose . . . with zero competition and constant forgiveness. When you live at this center-point, there's nothing beyond your reach . . . like the 'genie in the bottle', "your wish is the only command." Our prayer is that you find your way to this center-point of your life; that you live in a miracle-based environment of synchronicity, and that you defer all of the glory to that which G.enerates-O.ganizes-D.elivers the magic in your miracles . . . experience the experience of the "time of your life" with all of the time in your life.

All life is a commons -- there's a common thread that runs through all that is living, and the sensation of this connection is the sensation of love. The sensation of love is not a sense of emotional need, or its satisfaction -- it's a sense of devotion that's experienced when there's no other experience blocking its view . . . no need to be satisfied. The experience of love is not the experience of ownership, or exclusivity -- it's the experience of commonality and inclusion; of a sharing that's always been shared, and a cooperation at a level below the level of the actual experience. It's a sensation that can never abandon you; it's so foundational that it's not even the foundation . . . it's the earth, sand and gravel below it . . . even the thoughts of the ideas before the earth, sand and gravel ever existed. This is how close to the core the sensation of love and connection are, and the gift of this experience is honored in gratitude. This is why gratitude allows you to experience connection and love. In this experience you've entered the realm of synchronicity -- the realm where you ride on the source 'code-tales' of all existence, through the 'breath-trails' of all life . . . acting out stories from forever that make up the you in you. It's essential to purify these stories with the integrity of your intention; to recall this integrity as you deliver each moment. The great masters whisper words of encouragement if you're consciously listening. These words will purify the moments, they've existed forever. Angels repeat this encouragement with their songs beyond lifetimes, and the winds in the leaves with the rains on the winds all continue resounding this endless encouragement. It reminds life to experience connection . . . it reminds life that this experience of connection is love. Our prayer is that you embrace these threads that are common . . . the marriage of life without separation through the history of forever; that you value this embrace beyond your existence, and give thanks for the gift as the experience unfolds . . . this is the commons . . . this is the path of love . . . this will deliver the love of your life to the love in your life.

*R*iding on the 'code-tales' of existence, through the 'breath-trails' of your life, there are deep cellular memories -- stories from long before "ago" -- whose parts you've encountered through the chronology of lifetimes. This can assist your final assault on the highest mountain of your purpose . . . liberation from the cycles of birthing and dying. Within these 'tales' are the 'codes' -- the lessons you've encountered both cosmologically and genealogically. Lifetimes of 'in-spirit-tional' trial and error are combined with the parts that you've physically encountered, but never personally encountered . . . the ancestral codes in the DNA of your lineage. In this way, and in this very moment, your lineage is focused on the path of your legacy . . . seven generations of ancestors are all assisting your efforts as you climb this "mountain" breath by breath. The great masters are whispering in your ears with each breath of the climb, "Don't leave this mountain before you make your impression . . . place the imprint of your life on the legacy of Earth . . . for the only thing that matters to eternity, is the memory of you." With all of your ancestors helping, and with the masters by your side, the chances are very good that now is the time to start making such a difference; that now is the time to accumulate your memory and engage this great story. And in the midst of all this, hold firm to the values that do make a difference, for values are like the soul -- they're a never ending common thread that perfectly weaves your life into the fabric of time. Values enter with the breath -- they capture your 'thought-voice' echoing in the throat, and ride the breath into your heart . . . and from there into each cell. These values mix with those 'code-tales'

in your cellular memory to design the patterns through which your life expresses itself. Our prayer is that, in the midst of all this, you're constantly conscious; your awake to the process and connecting with each step; that you realize it's not random, but part of a much larger plan . . . and within all the stories, you locate a purpose for your life, right there, amongst the 'codes' in the 'tales'.

*Y*ogi Bhajan once said, "Convincing anyone that there's GOD, is like convincing someone that there's nothing at all. You can't experience it until you can; you don't know it until you do, and until this happens you have no idea what you're striving for, or if you are at all." Infinity is indescribable and undiscernible . . . it's like everything, and nothing. This is the nature of 'zero' and the nature of 'love' . . . an absolute constant that you're only able to experience when you're as consistent as it is. It's the parallel of, "Takes one to know one." This is life at its source -- the state of being simultaneously at ease and at zero . . . a state called 'shunya' by the yogic masters. The number -- or non-number -- of zero was discovered and introduced by the ancient Babylonians. A most important tool in mathematics, yet it was so threatening to all other formulas, that the Greeks placed a ban on it. The ancient masters of India worshipped it as the state of 'shunya' . . . the nothing in everything. It's a colorful history that's wound its way through the ages, but still . . . nevertheless . . . it's all about nothing. Zero is, in fact, the twin of infinity . . . nothing and everything existing within the same moment and space. It's in this state of nothing, of shunya, that you have the advantage of 'infinite-zero' -- you breathe the absolute newness of each moment . . . convincing your 'self' and ultimately your 'cells' -- in this rare state -- that time is born every moment. Under this influence -- like a magic spell -- the brain increases its hormone levels for acuity of vision while interpreting the surroundings. This removes the fog of uncertainty and all insecurity, and over time, produces a profoundly safe mood. In safety, the intuition opens to the time before and after time, for like zero -- a continuous loop -- time is a continuum . . . going around to come around. Our prayer is that you breathe yourself into this exalted state on a daily basis; that you become the absolute zero of shunya and enjoy the vast sense of safety; that you allow your intuition to replace all the mysteries, and trade in your limits for infinity . . . you are who you are.

When you completely surrender into your destiny, you'll experience a loft beneath your being -- like a wind beneath the wings of your life. The visceral explanation -- the body's response to this feeling -- is a profound freedom that you've only experienced at your own moment of birth . . . a strange, foreign introduction into these four dimensions of spacetime and life. The loft beneath your body is a flying that feels like falling . . . a birthing that feels like dying. In the ancient "East" it was called "riding the dragon" . . . the indigenous people of the "West" called it "riding the stallion". In such moments the certainty of success mix chaotically with the thoughts of demise -- the combination of fulfilling every dream, and disappearing into oblivion 'haunt' in this chaos. This is what stands at the threshold of your surrender . . . you arrive at this level of fulfillment through countless lifetimes of deep longing . . . you've come home, but you've lost the wanting . . . the longing . . . the desires. This sense of lift is frighteningly strange, and the human tendency is to reach back into the more predictable sensations of wanting and desiring . . . a natural reflex to create that which will disengage the fulfillment, and re-engage the struggle. The countless reasons why success is no longer wanted, and the 'wanting' is your better friend, ricochet throughout your thoughts and feelings. Convincing reasons why surrendering is worse than foolish, flash within your mind. This is the origin of "original sin" to the Christians, and the "fraud factor" to the Vedic yogis, where fulfillment is such a shock to the system, that the brain translates this shock as you've done something "very wrong." Circumstances can then shapeshift to confirm this "fact" -- as failure is often plucked from the jaws of success in such moments. Our prayer is that you find the loft under your wings; that you feel the body of that terrifying dragon beneath your life and surrender through the fear; work with the success of its strange uplifting ways, and willingly ride the risk . . . accept the success . . . and fulfill the destiny of your 'forever'.

'Mystic revolutionaries' . . . 'cosmic re-evolutionaries' . . . you're the ones who promised before your life, to fulfill the destiny with your life. The callings to succeed, as well as the gentle failings when you try, are demonstrated in the frustrations you experience when you're not. Those subtle senses of emptiness you catch out of the corner of your heart; that loneliness you can suddenly experience in a crowded room, and the fact that there's nothing to fear, yet you're a little afraid . . . these are the gauges on the dashboard of your life . . . they act as sensations to guide you. These sensations indicate there's more to accomplish on the path of fulfilling your promise . . . even when you're not remembering any promises. These are the sensations that make the path of life uncomfortable . . . and the annoyances relentless . . . a force like gravity . . . invisible, constant, and always experienced as opposition, until you surrender to its guidance. Surrendering to gravity is when you're relaxed, or falling through space, and then the feeling is suddenly free, weightless, and perhaps afraid. Until this full-on surrender, you're the weight of your weight. This falling can be reinterpreted and re-experienced as flying . . . this is why they call it "falling in love" . . . it's surrendering to the forces that are pulling you together to fly fearlessly through life. What is this "falling" . . . "flying" . . . "fearless" condition of fully surrendering to your destiny and your promise? Who is this 'mystic revolutionary', the 'cosmic re-evolutionary' you were born to be? How far beyond the ledge of gravity do you have to step, in order to fulfill this promise of your life? Our prayer is that you're ready, willing, and able to discover this person with these answers right now;

that you wake up in the morning, not looking to be normal, but looking to fall in love with the assignment of your life; that you interpret the falling as flying, and the destination as your destiny, and appreciate the rewards of your weightless 'sky-flying' every day. This is you being you, and surrendering to right now . . . the best time for re-evolution . . . the sky has no limit.

There's an 'authentic relationship' within everyone with their own higher-self . . . a highly conscious part of you. This part of you has "intimate" relationships with everything else and everyone else's higher-self . . . knows the details of the inside . . . from the inside. It's like a community that's operating outside of your awareness, but inside your capacity to know, if you develop the skills to access it . . . then it opens like a book to be read. Although the information appears brand new, it's existed forever; it's connected through a vast network . . . a web . . . one that the ancients said, "Has no weaver." There are trillions upon trillions of invisible 'ectoplasmic' threads connecting throughout this web; running between lives in this moment, and between every one's every moment. Innocence places you at the center of this gigantic expedition, and this is why children are born innocent . . . they know all the connections without words. Innocence places you into the timeline of synchronicity . . . in the direct path of your wishes and goals. This is the opportunity that every child is born innocently to fulfill. Synchronicity is the nature of time, where everything is in motion to fulfill itself eventually. Innocence gives you access to the controls of eventually -- and measures the unfolding timeline of 'eventually'. When you realize that this current moment was contained -- with infinite options -- in the beginning of time; when you know scientifically, that gravity bends and shapes time throughout space, and space throughout time; when you know that your attitude controls the endless options of time . . . with this is mind, every moment is your opportunity to innocently begin at the beginning with gratitude. For all that's going into this moment can be accessed from the vast 'immeasurable' contained within your own higher-self. Our prayer is that you capture each opportunity at the beginning of every moment; that you 'willingly' co-ordinate the process with your gratitude to proceed; that you're moved by your courage; governed by your innocence, and reaching for this higher awareness with every breath you breathe.

*R*esponding to time with deep acuity . . . awareness that receives the subtler signals from vision, hearing, and tactile feelings as clairvoyance, clairaudience and clairsentience . . . this must become the minimum standard of sensitivity for navigating into the uncertain future. This describes an evolution of humans from being creatures living in violent hierarchies of burden and servitude . . . one that's been in place for thousands of years . . . to being servants of a higher awareness that serves every moment. This is human beings, being humane . . . being what's been evolving, but never realized, for all these millenniums. Because when you add up all the present advancements in science and all the technologies -- and combine this with the still primitive, non-advancements in human social behavior . . . you end up with an evolution of the most dangerous creature in existence . . . one who's causing all of the current violence, pollution, starvation, and destruction. In other words, the "smartest" creature on the planet is an "illness" on the Earth . . . this isn't acceptable. The new response to time will require these maximum levels of attention combined with "zero" emotional reaction . . . attention to the degree that exposes absolutely everything that's taking place, combined with a discipline of non-reaction . . . literally "zero" amounts of taking offense. Without this combination, humans become even more dangerous; every tool becomes weaponized; indiscriminant violence increases, and as Gandhi once said, "An eye for an eye, and the world ends up blind." Instead of technology for violence, humans are capable of using technology for compassion. And in order to achieve this wiser planet -- the brilliant inventors of solutions, the ones with the ideas of great value, will have to survive the present environments of deceit and corruption with resolve, but not reaction. Our prayer is that you are this brilliance; that you show up and keep up under the pressures of the assignment; that you advance the goal of compassion and wisdom in the face of all this corruption . . . and do it because you can . . . because it's your destiny.

*L*ike in a hologram -- this moment of today was contained within the beginning of the world. While a hologram is a two-dimensional object, it contains all the information necessary to appear in a three-dimensional view. This is the nature of your higher consciousness . . . it's a holographic means of deriving more complex views from the next dimension to work within this one. Using your higher consciousness, you're able to untangle the entangled particles from the next dimensions, and formulate opportunities inside this dimension. Wouldn't you want to do this if you knew you could . . . wouldn't you want to participate in this world of miracles? This is a world that's available to anyone who has the will and the discipline to emerge from what is . . . to explore what is to be. This is the world of a very advanced magic, one that's derived from these current dimensions of logic. For the purpose of growth, this is the way a young child observes its surroundings; for the purpose of the next generation, this is the way a pregnancy occurs in the womb; for the purpose of blossoming, this is the way the bud views the moment. As with a bud, you must remember, it's time that allows the blossom to flower . . . from a willingness and hope that ignites it. Willingness and hope are connected to each other through your belief in the future -- the moments beyond this fourth dimension of time -- to allow the hologram of what is to be, to appear in the higher consciousness of this moment. Patience is not waiting, patience is knowing . . . knowing this future view of the ultimate outcome [will] come . . . and spending the time for it to arrive. Our prayer is that you take, or make, the time in the deepest moments of your meditations, to experience the buds that exist for all your ideas, plans and goals; that you use the hologram within your human higher consciousness to view these buds as future blossoms; that you use the time contained within your emotions, thoughts, and feelings to draw the maps of this journey through time, from the buds to the blossoms, and then rejoice in the experience of the great moments and the terrible ones . . . the desired outcomes are just now coming.

*P*laying with and relating to young children expands your innocence; your innocence enables an openness, and this openness generates a sense of probability within the available possibilities. This is the neuro-structure of a child's growth cycle; the way in which a child is stimulated to meet the daring challenges that require change, and the way the exact changes are selected to produce an accuracy for growing through time. This is also the structure at the core of the quantum world, at the source of all manifestation. Here, the actual particles of matter seem to not matter . . . they're mutable, they're like a child's decisions . . . they omni-locate all the time. The quantum attitude of these particles is an entanglement. This entanglement of quarks in the four-dimensions of spacetime has been mapped, through three dimensions of space and the fourth dimension of time. Gravity is believed to exist in a dimension just beyond this . . . the fifth dimension. According to Einstein's laws, gravity "bends" and "shapes" spacetime from this vantage in the fifth dimension, where a geometry emerges between these entangled quarks known as holographic-duality . . . the particles are so strongly interacting that they lose their individuality . . . they overlap in particle swarms that are actually existing everywhere at once. Masters in the ancient times referred to this as the omnipresence of manifesting spirit . . . the sadhus reveled in being one with this state . . . the transcendence of the worlds beyond this world. They referred to this location as the fifth element . . . the element of Ether. They said, "Whatever happens on the Earth, happens first in the Ether." This is the nature of innocence; the nature of a child's brain-mind connection that's constantly accessing this omni-locating, holographic-duality, which hasn't yet learned to believe in limitations. Our prayer is that you live part of your life in this child-like innocence; that you grow into your goals as a child grows into life; that you use this holographic-duality as a way of deriving more complex probabilities from the simple possibilities that are always in front of you . . . be the change you want to see in the world and become your future now.

*L*ife exists in an ocean of love . . . the ancient masters referred to this as Narayan. Your life is built on this love, and filled with opportunities to be aware of the universal connection it inspires. This connection is in every relation -- but it's not personal, or conditional -- the connection is a constant . . . just like love. Weighing and measuring the personalities, opinions and attitudes is a relation; it's entertaining, but -- if not disciplined -- it will displace the awareness of the connection, and then love is interpreted as conditional. This is the turbulent path in which most relations live and die with all of their opinions and interpretations, as the desire for entertainment outpaces the discipline for awareness. These relational opinions and interpretations are the conditional perceptions, negotiated contracts, and entertainment factors between personalities. These are not constant, nor are they permanent . . . they're the emotional content of passing moments. Authentic relations are based -- not on the contracts -- but on the awareness of the constants . . . the love and connection that nourishes life and flourishes with everything around it. In order for a relation to survive throughout time . . . to actually survive forever it must have this awareness as its primary focus, not the entertainment being worked on and struggled through. This is a personal commitment and can be individually applied . . . it will ultimately inspire a mutual reality . . . either participant in a relation can lead the way. As long as one participant is committed to maintaining their higher awareness, the realization of these universal principles of love and connection can be shared. Such relations sustain beyond death . . . beyond the adventure of their physical bodies and the measurement of the spacetime they exist in. Our prayer is that you develop such an awareness of the love and connection that's always present; that you have the discipline to understand that relations are interpretations, and while you allow these interpretations to change over time, and entertain you in the moment, you never lose track of the constant connection and the universal love.

*E*very morning, as you awaken, don't accept the attitude that sleep has delivered . . . it's incomplete. Meditate in the algorithms of your 'theta-brain', the post-dreamtime mind, and discover openings in the patterns that surround you . . . they're always there . . . this awakening neurology can discover them. The first meal of the day is called breakfast and it means: breaking the fast. There's a new medical revolution that's finding the health of your brain, to an extraordinary degree, is dictated by the state of your micro-biome -- the micro-organisms that live in your body and dramatically outnumber your own body cells. What takes place in your intestines determines how your brain functions. Early in the morning, before breaking the fast, this environment is more empty, calm and pliable -- you're able to translate thoughts and impressions more accurately in the quietness. As education attempts to train "normal" in a world of unique souls, it's trying to push water up a hill, but your early morning brain has the ability to understand your own personal 'normal' . . . you can find your 'self'. Surrendering into these dreamtime dimensions beyond spacetime, you access advantages in the early morning angles of your brain that don't occur at any other time. This allows you to alter your morning view; to further discover your life's 'masterplan', and align with it. If you don't have such a plan, you'll discover one . . . morning is the time. Once you have this plan in mind, you can alter it at any time -- it's a position to use as a 'touchstone' -- to sort through your life. Not every thought must be exactly aligned, but let them prove their value over time. Our prayer is that you give yourself the opportunity to have this internal process each morning; make this the beginning of your day before breaking your fast . . . experience the real practicality of meditation. Build on this inner-structure day after day, and as your 'masterplan' unfolds, remember, there will always be opposition -- that's the nature of nature working at the crack of dawn. Gently slip through the crack . . . shape your 'masterplan' . . . begin to live your very own life.

*Y*ou're living on planet Earth, a human being becoming more conscious of the Universe, and when you're aware that total synchronicity persists throughout the multi-verse -- an extraordinary electro-chemical shift takes place in your life . . . one that reveals the physical ease, emotional joy, mental knowing, and total sense of liberation at the very core of your being. A life of great potential unfolds . . . you become a human being, being humane; fulfilling your potential; living life on purpose . . . an extraordinary state. Why do so few live in this reality? It's the evolution of education and this is your future . . . the missing curriculums of mastery. Are children, today, taught how to respond to challenging moments with awareness, or emotions? Are they taught how matter and life are naturally synchronized, or randomly chaotic? Are they taught that this synchronicity is safety, or that life is dangerous? Trust isn't fully explained in any moment; faith is not taught except with conditions; synchronicity isn't demonstrated in history, or expected in the future. No one shows this because no one knows this . . . the blind lead the blind, and it's an eye for an eye world. There's greater opportunity for life where intuitive awareness allows grace to replace these instincts of fear, competition, and the violence based marketplace with its barbaric protection of territory. Economics becomes value based, not debt with burden; the ecology flourishes within this fearless abundance, not the fearful lack and scarcity. All of this is just below the false surface of your current human awareness. Look inside your world -- look at what else is taking place in your life -- experience the joy of your blood; the beat of your heart; the millions of cells reproducing every moment . . . the pulses, rhythms, and melodies of ease, joy, knowing and liberation. Our prayer is that you pause for a few moments -- every day -- and take stock; become aware of what's really going on beneath the surface of your world; embrace the wonders of life and allow them to hug you back . . . place pause in your world . . . breathe . . . pulsate . . . flourish, and be grateful.

*T*he human brain-mind connection has been freed from the preset angles of instinct, the angles that govern the entire animal kingdom. This is the preprogrammed behavior that aligns all other species with nature and the environment. Humans have the freedom to participate with nature, but not be controlled by it as they wend their way through lifetimes of trial and error to arrive in the higher nature . . . mastery with existence. Here on Earth, these trials have accelerated, as humans' battle the need to align with nature at all. "Why not just take advantage of it?" is the common question of "progress". The frustration and confusion that this misalignment generates, comes from the core of matter itself. Matter has been created by, and is maintained by, the universal tension, pressure, stress and friction. When you're aligned, you don't experience these challenging and chaotic qualities, but when you step out of alignment, these qualities dominate your life. Mastery is the evolutionary goal here; mastery comes as an ability to work and live in the matter of spacetime, while periodically washing away the collective frustration, confusion and misalignment that permeates the human version of life. This is achieved by dipping into the quantum "soup" that sits beneath the surface of these three dimensions of space and the fourth dimension of time. This is what your meditation time is designed to achieve -- to break the collective patterns of muddled logic, and be guided by quantum "soup" toward your desired outcomes . . . all the while dealing with the contagion of human thought "salad" and its muddled misalignment. That which is called mental disorders, in the current world, are simply advanced minds wildly searching for greater solutions in the quantum soup . . . and becoming lost in between the quantum and spacetime. The key is to establish a healthy cycle of time spent in the "soup" and time spent in the "salad". Our prayer is that you establish such a cycle on a daily basis; recharge yourself in the meditative quantum, and discharge yourself in the activity of spacetime; learn your natural rhythms . . . they'll assist you in becoming a mastery in the mystery.

*C*onscious mastery uses the tools of the emotional resources, interactive intelligence, and the intuition to solve the mysteries of each moment. In order to use these in their proper proportions, you must balance their overriding influences in the moments of charged activity. Emotions without the balance of intelligence are disruptive. Intelligence without the kindness of emotions is cold and aloof. Intuition without both interactive intelligence and the emotional resources will come off as unbelievable . . . like "wu-wu". This requires education, and true education produces true mastery. Today's educational environment is deeply competitive and unbalanced. It's producing reactions, so severe, their being labeled as disorders . . . the actual disorder is the system. Each child is to be balanced, treated with great respect in the first place, and delivered the curriculum of instructions secondarily. When a child feels respected for who they actually are; recognized for what they have to offer; approached with the individual care they deserve as a unique life, then they respond to education with their innate brilliance of learning. They're open to the information, because they realize how they can apply it . . . to improve their world, and the world. This is the inclusiveness of conscious education, it educates the emotional resources; the interactive intelligence, and the higher intuition all at once. The beauty of intuition is that every child is born with this as their strongest resource. It's the nature of survival, but it's being stripped away with other emphasis as the child grows older. Current education does not honor or recognize this power, and even dismisses it as daydreaming, or worse, as an attention disorder. Our prayer is that you approach the children of this world, no matter what their age . . . zero to a hundred, and honor the brilliance they've brought in their own unique way; set an example of how the world prospers from their exceptional value and contribution; create a new normal that includes every unique skill . . . enable the masters as they learn their way to mastery.

The power of eventually, which is a product of eternity, which is a product of infinity -- in which there are no laws -- is that everything can happen eventually. As the saying goes, "Where there's a will, there's a way," -- therefore logically means . . . if it can happen . . . when there's a will -- it will happen . . . eventually. Since eventually says that everything can happen . . . the will is accurate and authorized to say, "Everything will happen." The only variable for which you are responsible for in your life is -- how long will 'eventually' take . . . when is now a good time? This is the universal magic that interfaces with the universal logic, allowing for a balance between the two -- the yin and the yang. With a slight lean from this perfect balance toward your will, it initiates motion, which generates all the outcomes. Einstein found that time is just space moving through a point of perception. There's an argument that entertains the science of physics. "Is it the space, or is it the point of perception that's actually moving? Either way, the space exists before it's been perceived, but until it's perceived it remains invisibly in the future reference of time. And the space that has already passed through the point of perception -- known as the past . . . also still exists. It becomes obvious from this realization that both future and past are in continuous existence, even when they're outside the experience of perception. This plays into the outstanding advantage of human consciousness and its connection with the power of eventually. It's yours to work with if you take advantage of this human advantage. Our prayer is that you relate to the universal magic that balances the universal logic; that you take advantage of the advantages of being human; that you live outside the instinctual limits of pure logic, and ride the waves of time at their point of balance . . . perceive the present, future and past as a continuum, and live in the experience of your own will without attachments. Lean into your will from this point of pure balance and every dream [will] eventually come into the present . . . now is a good time for now.

*T*his moment -- in every possible way -- is entering your psyche through your sensory system; entering through your memory system; entering through emotionally creative system to assist the accumulation of your perspectives of everything. All that you've experienced in every lifetime -- as well as this one -- is the code that's translating into your cognitive experience. It's all available as a vital part of what you're working with . . . all of your beliefs and disbeliefs. This code receives guidance from your desires . . . they will either move you forward into the present experience, or remove you from it. You're higher desires guide you forward into the present . . . your lower desires guide you backward into your memory. Sometimes it's necessary to go back, in order to get your feet on the ground, by remembering the great lessons in your failures . . . at other times it's necessary to reach out into the vastness of the unknown future and experience that which is beyond your recollection . . . a future memory of the collective recollection. And so the play of life unfolds within you, before you, and because of you, and as this play unfolds, you enter every room as the main character. Even when your role is in a supporting position to the story of the moment, you're still the main character of your life. Therefore, whenever you enter a room make it your home, and then enable everyone else in the room to feel at home. Enter the space that's not yet occupied, so you can gain access to the time that does not yet exist. This may appear like nonsense, but when you dig deeper into your senses; as you go further into memory and future-memory; as you experience more profoundly the creativity of your intuition, you're giving yourself the opportunity to transform spacetime . . . to become that true alchemist. Our prayer is that you ride the code of your life on this journey; that you take hold of the wheel like it's yours; let the unknown nature of spacetime be your inspiration that ignites enthusiasm, and let this enthusiasm drive the story forward through your human experience . . . ride it like you own it.

Time is a wave in the fabric of space, and every wave is a cycle. Everything that's affected by time has cycles. The cycles of all matter have created it, and are determined to recycle it. The word recycle means to continue the cycle that exists in the waves of time. Ferrous metals have rust; wood has decay and rot; stones and minerals have the dissolving effects of winds, water and time. Organic bodies are made up of many elements and experience the effects of all these processes. The rusting is call oxidation, the decaying, dissolving and rot are called aging and gravity, and when they accelerate they're called disease and disorder. Even ideas are faced with the recycling oppositions of doubt and decay; they're only as strong as their ability to withstand the tests of time. All of this is the cycling and recycling of nature . . . of time. When anything is important to those who possess it -- whether virtual, like an idea, or actual, like substance -- when something is considered of great value, there are efforts put in play to protect this value from the natural recycling processes. And at the same time these natural processes are also extremely valuable -- they continuously clean and clear away anything that's not protected. This is why when you possess importance, you must protect it with your physical discipline; value it with your thoughts and emotions. One version of prayer is to reaffirm the value of your valuables . . . the lives and environments that are dear to you. This is also the process of your auto-immune system's protection . . . and your awareness that prevents accidents. You increase your power to maintain value by enhancing awareness attitudes; by producing levitational emotions, and by constructing thoughts that believe in strengths and deflect the natural doubts. Our prayer is that you protect everything and everyone that's valuable to you with a concerted effort of thought, prayer, emotion and habit; that you allow doubt to recycle the debris, but remove it from your valuables; that you focus your time and value your life consciously . . . this is the tuning up with and synchronizing to the nature of time that produces the extraordinary.

Our Prayer

We are inspired with the opportunity to serve you in this way -- contributing enlightened words into the conversations, connection's and challenges of everyday life. We are dedicated to explaining the confusing and unknown in a meaningful and practical way, and to provide this information for those who seek a brighter, sustainable and prosperous future. We are grateful for your participation in this process, made obvious by the very fact that you're reading this page right now.

In addition to these written words, we offer our musical CD's of meditation mantras; podcasts of our group Kundalini yoga and Humanology classes and lectures; video classes of Kundalini yoga sets (both short form and long) to be done on your own; workshops around the world to join others just like you, and many other products.

To find out about all of this and more, please visit us online. Bless you for all that you do . . . in all the ways that you are able.

With Deep Gratitude . . . The Team at GuruSingh.com

Website: www.gurusingh.com
Twitter: @gurusingh
Twitter: @gurusinghdaily
Instagram: @gurusinghyogi
Facebook: Guru Singh Daily https://www.facebook.com/Gurusingh
daily/

NOTES:

NOTES:

NOTES:

49699005R00162

Made in the USA
San Bernardino, CA
02 June 2017